1.95

CW00649848

The Message of Islam

❖ Wisdom of the East Series ❖

The Message of Islam

*Being a résumé of the teaching of the Qur-an:
with special reference to the spiritual and moral
struggles of the human soul*

*by A. Yusuf Ali, C.B.E., M.A.,
LL.M. (Cantab.), F.R.S.L.*

John Murray
London

© This edition 1992

First published in 1940
by John Murray (Publishers) Ltd,
50 Albemarle Street, London W1X 4BD

All rights reserved.
Unauthorised duplication contravenes applicable laws.

A catalogue record of this book is available from
the British Library.

ISBN 0-7195-5140-4

PRINTED IN THE UNITED STATES

FOREWORD

As a humble Muslim and a devout believer in the unity of God and the universality of His Message, I have tried to interpret the Qur-ān in the English language. In a complete translation with the Text and a full Commentary, the work occupies 1,849 large pages. In order to help such readers as were unfamiliar with the subject, or wished to get a bird's-eye view without going into details of scholarship, history, or theology, a rhythmic running commentary was included in the scheme, which summarised the main teaching of the Book in short paragraphs of free verse. These have been much appreciated, and a desire was expressed that they should be published separately, in a small volume, which would render them accessible to the general reader.

This has now been done. To meet the exigencies of space, the form of free verse has been discarded, and the whole has been printed in the form of prose, which may possibly make a better appeal to modern readers.

The attainment of a universal human brotherhood may in present circumstances seem to many to be a distant ideal. But it is worth working for. It can only be done by pooling our spiritual resources. In the words of paragraph 64,

> " Keep together in your noble Brotherhood ;
> Share its joys and sorrows ;
> Strive and fight the good fight,
> And fear not."

A. YUSUF ALI.

LONDON.
August 12, 1939.

EDITORIAL NOTE

MY object as editor of this series is a very definite one. I desire above all things that these books shall be ambassadors of goodwill between East and West. I hope that they will contribute to a fuller knowledge of the great cultural heritage of the East, for only through real understanding will the West be able to appreciate the underlying problems and aspirations of Asia today. I am confident that a deeper knowledge of the great ideals and lofty philosophy of Eastern thought will help to a revival of that true spirit of charity which neither despises nor fears the nations of another creed and colour.

J. L. CRANMER-BYNG

CONTENTS

INTRODUCTION

God's Purpose with Man

1. Glory to God Most High, full of Grace and Mercy ;
He created All, including Man.

To Man He gave a special place in His Creation.

He honoured man to be His Agent, and to that end,
endued him with understanding, purified his affections, and
gave him spiritual insight ;

So that Man should understand Nature, understand himself, and know God through His wondrous Signs, and
glorify Him in truth, reverence, and unity.

2. For the fulfilment of this great trust Man was further
given a Will,

So that his acts should reflect God's universal Will and
Law, and his mind, freely choosing, should experience the
sublime joy of being in harmony with the Infinite, and with
the great drama of the world around him, and with his own
spiritual growth.

3. But, created though he was in the best of moulds, Man
fell from Unity when his Will was warped, and he chose
the crooked path of Discord.

And sorrow and pain, selfishness and degradation, ignorance
and hatred, despair and unbelief poisoned his life,

And he saw shapes of evil in the physical, moral, and spiritual world, and in himself.

4. Then did his soul rise against himself, and his self-discord made discord between kith and kin :

Men began to fear the strong and oppress the weak, to boast in prosperity, and curse in adversity, and to flee each other, pursuing phantoms,

For the truth and reality of Unity was gone from their minds.

5. When men spread themselves over the earth, and became many nations, speaking diverse languages, and observing diverse customs and laws ;

The evils became multiplied, as one race or nation became alienated from another.

The Brotherhood of Man was now doubly forgotten,— first, between individuals, and secondly, between nations.

Arrogance, selfishness, and untruth were sown and reaped in larger fields ;

And Peace, Faith, Love, and Justice were obscured over masses of men, as large tracts of land are starved of sunshine by clouds floating far on high.

6. But God in His infinite mercy and love, Who forgives and guides individuals and nations and turns to good even what seems to us evil, never forsakes the struggling soul that turns to Him,

Nor the groups of men and women who join together to obey His Will and Law and strengthen each other in unity and truth,

Nor the Nations that dwell in mountain or valley, heat or cold, in regions fertile or arid,

In societies that roam over land or seas, or hunt, or tend flocks, or till the soil, or seek the seas for food or oil, or fat, or gems,

Or dig out from the bowels of the earth precious stones, or metals or stored-up heat and energy, or practise arts and crafts, or produce abundant wealth by machines of ingenious workmanship,

Or live a frugal life of contemplation :

For all are children of One God,

And share his loving care and must be brought within the pale of His eternal unity and harmony.

The Light of His Revelation

7. And so this light of eternal Unity has shone in all ages and among all nations,

Through chosen Apostles of God, who came as men to dwell among men,

To share their joys and sorrows, to suffer for them and with them,—

Aye, and to suffer more than falls to ordinary mortal lot,—

That so their message and their life might fulfil the eternal and unchanging purpose of the Most High,—

To lead man to his noblest destiny.

8. Ever this eternal light of Unity, this mystic light of God's own Will, has shone and shines with undiminished splendour.

The names of many Messengers are inscribed in the records of many nations and many tongues,

And many were the forms in which their message was delivered

According to the needs of the time and the understanding of the people ;

And manifold were the lives of the Messengers, and manifold also was the response of their people ;

But they all witnessed to the One Truth : of God's unity, might, grace, and love.

9. As the records of man are imperfect, and the memory of man unstable :

The names of many of these messengers are known in one place and not in another, or among one people and not among others ;

And some of their names may have perished utterly ;

But their message stands one and indivisible,

Even though it may have been forgotten, or twisted by ignorance, error, superstition, or perversity ;

Or misunderstood in the blinding light of time or tortuous Circumstance.

10. Many were the faiths in the composite world of Western Asia, Northern Africa, and Europe,

And many were the fragments of ancient wisdom, saved, transformed, renewed, or mingled ;

And many new streams of wisdom were poured through the crucibles of noble minds,—prophets, poets, preachers, philosophers, and thinking men of action ;

And many were the conflicts, and many the noble attempts reaching out towards Unity,

And many were the subtle influences interchanged with the other worlds of further and Eastern Asia,—

Aye, and perchance with the scattered Isles of the Pacific and the world between the Atlantic and the Pacific.

The Voice of Unity

11. At length came the time when the Voice of Unity should speak and declare to the People,

Without the need of Priests or Priest-craft,

Without miracles save those that happen now and always in the spiritual world,

Without mystery, save those mysteries which unfold themselves in the growing inner experience of man and his vision of God,—

To declare with unfaltering voice the Unity of God, the Brotherhood of Man,

And Grace and Mercy, Bounty and Love, poured out in unstinted measure for ever and ever.

12. And this great healing light shone among a people steeped in ignorance,

Brave and free, but without cohesion or union,

Simple and rude, but with an easy familiarity with Nature,

Accustomed to Nature's hardships and her rugged resistance to man, but dreaming of the delights of gardens and fruitful fields,

Cruel, yet with a rough sense of equality,

And wielding a tongue, flexible, beautiful, and able to respond, with brevity and eloquence, to the sublimest thoughts which man could conceive.

13. Who were fit to be vehicles of this light ?—

Not men intoxicated with words and mysteries,

Men whom politics had debauched or tyranny had subdued,

Men whose refinement had ended in vices,

Who saw Nature only through books or artificial conceits, or in moods which bred softness, indolence, or luxury,

Who spoke of love and justice, but practised gross selfishness between class and class, sex and sex, condition and condition ;

And had perverted their language, once beautiful, into jargons of empty elegance and unmeaning futility.

14. For the glory of Hellas, and her freedom and wisdom had departed ;

Rome's great systems of law, organisation, and universal citizenship had sunk into the mire of ecclesiastical formalism, and dogmatism, and exclusive arrogance ;

The living fire of Persia's Prophet scarce smouldered in her votaries of luxury ;

In India, countless castes and kingdoms cancelled the unity of Buddha's teaching ;

The wounds of China had not yet been healed by T'ang culture ;

And Japan was still a disciple of China.

15. Then, in the sacred city of pagan Arabia, shone a light that spread in all directions.

It was centrally placed for the bounds of the world of men's habitations in Asia, Europe, and Africa.

It made the Arabs the leading nation of culture and science, of organised enterprise, law, and arts,

With a zeal for the conquest of Nature and her mysteries.

Muhammad

16. Behold ! There was born into the world of sense the unlettered Apostle,

The comely child, noble of birth, but nobler still in the grace and wisdom of human love and human understanding ;

Dowered with the key which opened to him the enchanted palace of nature ;

Marked out to receive—to receive and preach in burning words the spiritual truth and message of the Most High.

17. Others before had been born in darkness, beyond the reach of history ;

Others again it pleased God to send as Messengers, preaching, working in the dim twilight of history,

Wherein men fashion legends after their own hearts, and dimly seek a light afar, remote from lives mean and sordid, such as they knew.

18. But Muhammad came in the fullest blaze of history ;

With no learning he put to shame the wisdom of the learned ;

With pasture folk he lived and worked, and won their love ;

In hills and valleys, caves and deserts, he wandered, but never lost his way to truth and righteousness ;

From his pure and spotless heart the Angels washed off the dust that flew around him ;

Through the ways of crooked city folk, he walked upright and straight,

And won from them the ungrudging name of the Man of Faith [1] who never broke his word.

19. To the Praiseworthy [2] indeed be praise :
Born in the Sacred City, [3] he destroyed its superstition ;
Loyal to his people to the core, he stood for all humanity ;
Orphan-born and poor, he envied not the rich, and made his special care all those whom the world neglected or oppressed,—
Orphans, women, slaves, and those in need of food or comforts, mental solace, spiritual strength, or virtues downtrodden in the haunts of men.

20. His mother [4] and his foster-mother [5] loved and wondered at the child ;
His grandfather, 'Abdul Muṭṭalib, of all his twice-eight children and their offspring, loved him best, and all his sweet and gentle ways ;
His uncle Abū Ṭālib, loth though he was to give up the cult of his fathers, knew well the purity of Muḥammad's mind and soul,
And was his stoutest champion when the other chiefs of Mecca sought to kill the man who challenged in his person their narrow Pagan selfish lives.

21. To his cousin 'Ali, the well-beloved, [6] born when he was thirty,

[1] Al-Amīn.   [2] Muḥammad.   [3] Mecca.   [4] Āmina.
[5] Ḥalīma.   [6] Murtadhā.

16

He appeared as the very pattern of a perfect man,

As gentle as he was wise and true and strong,

The one in whose defence and aid he spent his utmost strength and skill,

Holding life cheap in support of a cause so high,

And placing without reserve his chivalry, his prowess, wit, and learning, and his sword at the service of this mighty Messenger of God.

His Mission

22. Not till the age of forty [1] did he receive the Commission

To stand forth and proclaim the Bounty of God,

And His gift, to lowly Man, of knowledge by Word and Pen ;

But all through his years of preparation he did search the Truth ;

He sought it in Nature's forms and laws, her beauty and her stern unflinching ways ;

He sought it in the inner world of human lives,

Men's joys and sorrows, their kindly virtues and their sins of pride, injustice, cruel wrong, and greed of gain, scarce checked by the inner voice

That spoke of duty, moral law, and higher still, the Will Supreme of God, to which the will of man must tune itself to find its highest bliss.

23. But as he grew, steadfast in virtue and purity,

Untaught by men, he learnt from them, and learned to teach them ;

[1] The Arabian year before A.H. 10 was roughly luni-solar.

Even as a boy of nine, when he went in a trade caravan with Abu Tālib to Syria,[1]

His tender soul marked inwardly how God did speak,

In the wide expanse of deserts, in the stern grandeur of rocks, in the refreshing flow of streams, in the smiling bloom of gardens, in the art and skill with which men and birds and all life sought for light

From the Life of Lives, even as every plant seeks through devious ways the light of the Sun.

24. Nor less was he grieved at Man's ingratitude

When he rebelled and held as naught the Signs of God, and turned His gifts to baser uses,

Driving rarer souls to hermit life,

Clouding the heavenly mirror of pure affections with selfish passions, mad unseemly wrangles, and hard unhallowed loathsome tortures of themselves.

25. He worked and joyed in honest labour ;

He traded with integrity to himself and to others ;

He joined the throngs of cities and their busy life, but saw its good and evil as types of an inner and more lasting life hereafter ;

People gladly sought his help as umpire and peacemaker because they knew his soul was just and righteous ;

He loved the company of old and young, but oft withdrew to solitude for Prayer and inward spiritual strength ;

He despised not wealth but used it for others ;

---

[1] It was on such visits that he met and conversed with Nestorian Christian Monks like Bahīra, who were quick to recognise his spiritual worth.

18

He was happy in poverty and used it as his badge and his pride,[1]

When wealth was within his reach but not within his grasp,

As a man among men.

26. At twenty-five he was united in the holy bonds of wedlock with Khadīja the Great,

The noble lady who befriended him when he had no worldly resources,

Trusted him when his worth was little known,

Encouraged and understood him in his spiritual struggles,

Believed in him when with trembling steps he took up the Call

And withstood obloquy, persecution, insults, threats, and tortures,

And was a life-long help-mate till she was gathered to the saints in his fifty-first year,—

A perfect woman, the mother of those that believe.

27. There is a cave in the side of Mount Hiraa some three miles north of the City of Mecca,

In a valley which turns left from the road to 'Arafāt,

To which Muḥammad used to retire for peaceful contemplation :

Often alone, but sometimes with Khadīja.

Days and nights he spent there with his Lord.

Hard were the problems he revolved in his mind,—

Harder and more cross-grained than the red granite of the rock around him,—

[1] " Poverty is my Pride " : a saying of the Prophet.

Problems not his own, but his people's,

Yea, and of human destiny, of the mercy of God, and the age-long conflict of evil and righteousness, sin and abounding Grace.

28. Not till forty years of earthly life had passed

Was the veil lifted from the Preserved Tablet

And its contents began to be transferred to the tablet of his mind,

To be proclaimed to the world, and read and studied for all time,—

A fountain of mercy and wisdom, a warning to the heedless, a guide to the erring, an assurance to those in doubt, a solace to the suffering, a hope to those in despair,—

To complete the chain of Revelation through the mouths of divinely inspired Apostles.

29. The Chosen One [1] was in the Cave of Hiraa.

For two years and more he had prayed there and adored his Creator

And wondered at the mystery of man

With his corruptible flesh, just growing out of human seed, [2]

And the soul in him reaching out to knowledge sublime, new and ever new,

Taught by the bounty of God, and leading to that which man himself knoweth not.

And now behold ! a dazzling vision of beauty and light overpowered his senses, and he heard the word " *Iqraa !* "

[1] Mustafa.   [2] See Qur-ān, *S. 96*, 2.

30. "*Iqraa !* "—which being interpreted may mean "Read !" or "Proclaim !" or "Recite !".—

The unlettered Apostle was puzzled ; he could not read.

The Angel seemed to press him to his breast in a close embrace, and the cry rang clear, "*Iqraa !* "

And so it happened three times ;

Until the first overpowering sensation yielded to a collected grasp of the words which made clear his Mission ;

Its Author, God the Creator ;

Its subject, Man, God's wondrous handiwork, capable, by Grace, of rising to heights sublime ;

And the instrument of that mission, the sanctified Pen, and the sanctified Book, the Gift of God, which men might read, or write, or study, or treasure in their souls.

His First Disciples

31. The veil was lifted from the Chosen One's eyes.

And his soul for a moment was filled with divine ecstasy

* * *

When this passed, and he returned to the world of Time and Circumstance and this world of Sense,

He felt like one whose eyes had seen a light of dazzling beauty, and felt dazed on his return to common sights.

The darkness now seemed tenfold dark ;

The solitude seemed tenfold empty ;

The mount of Hiraa, henceforth known as the Mountain of Light, the mere shell of an intense memory.

Was it a dream ?

Terror seized his limbs and he straightway sought her who shared his inmost life, and told her of his sense of exaltation, and the awful void when the curtain closed.

32. She understood, rejoiced, and comforted him ;
Gave strength to his shaken senses ;
Wrapped up in warmth his shivering body, unused as
yet to bear the strain and stress of an experience rare to
mortal men.

She knew it was no dream or delusion.

She went and consulted her cousin Waraqa, a devout
worshipper of God in the Faith of Christ, learned in spiritual
lore.

He listened and with her rejoiced that he, Muḥammad, was
God's Chosen One to renew the Faith.

33. She said : " Blessed be thou, Chosen One !
" Do we not see thy inner life,—true and pure ?
" Do not all see thy outer life,—kind and gentle ?—
" Loyal to kin, hospitable to strangers ?
" No thought of harm or mischief ever stained thy mind,
" Nor word ever passed thy lips that was not true or
stilled not the passions of narrower men.
" Ever ready in the service of God, thou art he of whom
I bear witness :
" There's no God but He, and thou art His Chosen
Apostle."

34. Khadīja believed, exalted in faith above all women ;
' Alī, the well-beloved, then a child of ten, but lion-hearted,
plighted his faith, and became from that moment the right
hand of Islam ;

Abū Bakr, the Sincere,[1] the True-hearted, the man of
wealth and influence, who used both without stint for the

[1] A title of Abū Bakr.

Cause, the sober counsellor, the inseparable friend, never hesitated to declare his faith ;

And Zaid, the freedman of Muḥammad, counted his freedom as naught compared with the service of Muḥammad and Islam.

These were the first-fruits of the mission :

A woman, a child, a man of affairs, and a freedman, all banded together in the equality of Islam.

The Task before Him

35. The revelation had come, the mission and the inspiration. But what was it leading to ?

It was a miracle, but not in the sense of a reversing of Nature ;

Muṣṭafā's vision was linked with Eternity, but he was no soothsayer foretelling passing events ;

The mysteries of knowledge were being opened out, but his message was no mere esoteric doctrine, to be grasped by a few in contemplation, fleeing from action ;

Nor was it the practice of single or social monasticism, undisturbed by the whims or passions of life.

He was asked to stand forth, to preach, to declare the One Universal God, the Gracious, the Merciful,

And to lead men to the Right and forbid the Wrong.

36. The wrong ?— The selfish pride of birth,
The massing of power and wealth in the hands of a few,
The slaughter of female infants,
The orgies of gambling and drunkenness,
The frauds of temples and idols and priests,
The feuds and arrogance of tribes and races,

The separation of Sacred and Profane,
As if the unity of all Life and all Truth did not flow from the unity of God Most High.

37. He was loyal to his family, but could he support their monopoly of power ?—
To his tribe, but were the Quraish the only creatures of God ?—
To the temple of Mecca, but could he wink at Lāt and 'Uzzā, and the other monsters, whose worship killed the spiritual growth of Man ?—
To the earlier Revelations, but could he hold with the superstitions and falsehoods, the dogmas and creeds which went against reason and nature, and the inner light which was now fanned into flame by the Will of God ?

38. And so his very virtues and loyalties pointed to offence and conflict,
Mockery and misrepresentation, hatred and persecution,
Threats, tortures, and exile for him and his,
And martyrdoms, wars, revolutions, and the shaking of the foundations of history and the social order.
But Islam meant the willing submission of his will to God,
The active attainment of Peace through Conflict.

39. And he gave that submission, not without effort,
Even as Moses [1] did before him,
And Jesus [2] in the agony of the garden of Gethsemane.

*   *   *

[1] Qur-ān, S. *20*, 25–32.   [2] Matt. xxvi. 39.

40. For three and twenty years, in patience, conflict, hope,
and final triumph,
Did this man of God receive and teach the Message of the
Most High.
It came, like the fruit of the soul's own yearning, to teach
profound spiritual truths,
Answer questions, appeal to men in their doubts and fears,
Help and put heart in them in moments of trial,
And ordain for them laws by which they could live in
society lives of purity, goodness and peace.

41. These messages came as inspiration to Muḥammad
as the need arose, on different occasions and in different
places :
He recited them, and they were recorded by the Pen :
They were imprinted on his heart and mind, and on the
memory of his loving disciples :
As the body of sacred Scripture grew, it was arranged for
purposes of public prayer and reading :
This is the Book, or the Reading, or the Qur-ān.

THE QUR-ĀN

S. 1.   42. First comes that beautiful Sūra,[1] the Opening Chapter
of Seven Verses, rightly called the Essence of the Book.

It teaches us the perfect Prayer.

For if we can pray aright, it means that we have some
knowledge of God and His attributes, of His relations to us
and His creation, which includes ourselves ;

That we glimpse the source from which we come, and
that final goal which is our spiritual destiny under God's
true judgment :

Then we offer ourselves to God and seek His light.

43. Prayer is the heart of Religion and Faith.   But how
shall we pray ?

What words shall convey the yearnings of our miserable
ignorant hearts to the Knower of all ?

Is it worthy of Him or of our spiritual nature to ask for
vanities, or even for such physical needs as our daily bread ?

The Inspired One taught us a Prayer that sums up our
faith, our hope, and our aspiration in things that matter.

We think in devotion of God's name and His Nature ;

---

[1] Each "chapter" or division of the Qur-ān is called a Sūra, which
means a Degree or Step, by which we mount up.   Here the Sūras
are indicated as S.1, S.2, etc., down to S.114 at p. 123.

We praise Him for His creation and His cherishing care ;
We call to mind the Realities, seen and unseen ;
We offer Him worship and ask for His guidance ;
And we know the straight from the crooked path by the light of His grace that illumines the righteous.

MEN AND NATIONS

S. 2. 44. The Message of God is a guide that is sure to those who seek His light.

But those who reject faith are blind : their hearts are sealed.

Woe to the hypocrites, self-deceived and deceiving others,

With mockery on their lips, and mischief in their hearts, and fear ;

The clouds that bring fertilising rain to others, to them bring but deafening thunder-peals and lightning-flashes blinding to their eyes.

45. Yet man ! What wonderful destiny is thine !

Created to be God's vicegerent on earth ! A little higher than angels !

Yet beguiled by evil ! Set for a season, this earth's probationer, to purge thy stain,

With the promise of guidance and hope from on high, from the Oft-Returning, Merciful !

Wilt thou choose right and regain thy spiritual home with God ?

46. Amongst men what nation had higher chances in the realm of the Spirit than the Children of Israel ?

But again and again did they fail in the Spirit.

They rebelled against Moses and murmured in the wilderness ;

The Prophets they slew and the Signs they rejected ;

They falsified Scripture and turned their backs on righteousness.

47. The people of Moses and the people of Jesus were given revelations,

But alas ! they played false with their own lights, and in their selfishness, made narrow God's universal message.

To them it seemed incredible that His light should illumine Arabia and reform the world.

But His ways are wondrous, and they are clear to those who have Faith.

48. If the People of the Book rely upon Abraham, let them study his history.

His posterity included both Israel and Ismā'īl.

Abraham was a righteous man of God, a Muslim, and so were his children.

Abraham and Ismā'īl built the Ka'ba as the house of God and purified it, to be a centre of worship for all the world :

For God is the God of all Peoples.

49. But those people have passed away, who promised to uphold the Law of God.

Their progeny having been found unworthy, their place was taken by a new people looking towards Mecca,—

A new people, with a new Messenger,

To bear witness to God's Law, to proclaim the truth, maintain His symbols, and strive and fight for Unity in God's Way.

50. The Society thus organised must live under laws that would guide their every-day life,—

Based on eternal principles of righteousness and fair dealing, cleanliness and sobriety, honesty and helpfulness, one to another,—

Yet shaped into concrete forms, to suit times and circumstances, and the varying needs of average men and women :

The food to be clean and wholesome ; blood feuds to be abolished ; the rights and duties of heirs to be recognised after death, not in a spirit of Formalism, but to help the weak and the needy and check all selfish wrong-doing ;

Self-denial to be learnt by fasting ;

The courage to fight in defence of right, to be defined ;

The Pilgrimage to be sanctified as a symbol of unity ;

Charity and help to the poor to be organised ;

Unseemly riot and drink and gambling to be banished ;

Orphans to be protected ;

Marriage, divorce, and widowhood to be regulated ;

And the rights of women, apt to be trampled underfoot, now clearly affirmed.

51. Fighting in defence of Truth and Right is not to be undertaken light-heartedly, nor to be evaded as a duty.

Life and Death are in the hands of God.

Not all can be chosen to fight for God. It requires constancy, firmness, and faith.

Given these, large armies can be routed by those who battle for God,

As shown by the courage of David, whose prowess single-handed disposed of the Philistines.

The mission of some of the apostles, like Jesus, was different, —less wide in scope than that of Muṣṭafā.

God's plan is universal, and He carries it out as He wills.

GOD AND MAN

52. Who can describe the nature of God ?

The Living, the Eternal :

His Throne extends over worlds and worlds that no imagination can encompass.

His truth is clear as daylight :

How can compulsion advance Religion ?

The keys of Life and Death, and the mysteries of everything around us, are in His hands.

Our duty then is to seek the path of goodness, kindness, upright conduct and Charity,—

To grasp at no advantage from a brother's need, to stand by the word that is pledged, to bear true witness, and remove all cause of misunderstanding in our dealings as between man and man.

53. Our honesty and upright conduct are not mere matters of policy or convenience :

All our life in this world must be lived as in the presence of God.

The finest example of Faith we have in the Apostle's life :

Full of faith, let us render willing obedience to God's Will,

Our responsibility, though great, is not a burden greater than we can bear :

Let us pray for God's assistance, and He will help.

S. 3. 54. The Qur-ān revelation has, step by step, confirmed the Law of Moses and the Gospel of Jesus.

It is a guide from God, and appeals to reason and understanding.

Let us understand it rightly, in reverence and truth, unswayed by those who reject faith, and seeking ever the reward of the Pleasure of God, through firmness, patience, discipline, and charity, and offering others the light which we have ourselves received.

S. 3. 55. If the People who received earlier revelations confine themselves to partial truths, and in their pride shut their eyes to the whole of the Book of God, their day is done :

Let the Muslims seek the society and friendship of their own, and trust in God, who knows all, and holds every soul responsible for its own deeds.

56. God's truth is continuous, and His Apostles from Adam, through Noah and Abraham, down to the last of the Prophets, Muḥammad, form one brotherhood.

Of the progeny of 'Imrān, father of Moses and Aaron, sprang a woman, who devoted her unborn offspring to God.

The child was Mary the mother of Jesus.

Her cousin was the wife of the priest Zakarīyā, who took charge of Mary.

To Zakarīyā, in his old age, was born a son Yaḥyā, amid prodigies :

Yaḥyā was the herald of Jesus the son of Mary, and was known as John the Baptist.

Jesus was of virgin birth, and performed many miracles.

But those to whom he came as Prophet rejected him, and plotted for his death.

Their plots failed, for God's Plan is above man's plots.
So will it be with Islam, the Truth from all eternity.

57. Islam doth invite all people to the Truth : there is no cause for dissembling or disputing.

False are the people who corrupt God's truth, or hinder men from coming to God.

Let the Muslims hold together in unity and discipline, knowing that they have a mission of righteousness for humanity.

No harm can come to them.

Though there are good men and true in other Faiths, Muslims must be true to their own Brotherhood.

They should seek help and friendship from their own, and stand firm in constancy and patient perseverance.

58. God's help comes to those who strive with firmness, as it did at Badr.

Much can be learnt from the misfortunes at Uḥud.

It is not for us to question God's Plan, which is full of wisdom and mercy for all.

Our duty is to stand firm and unswerving, to obey, and in steadfast courage to persevere, to retrieve our mistakes, not in grief and despair, but in firm hope in God and in contempt of pain and death.

MAN TO BE FIRM AND TO TRUST IN GOD

59. Uḥud showed how dangerous it was to lend ear to enemy suggestions, to disobey orders, dispute, lose courage, or seek selfish ends ; some even followed the evil course of turning back.

But great is God's mercy : where He helps, no harm can come.

Trust your Leader.

The Hypocrites, in withdrawing from battle, were really helping the Unbelievers, but glorious were those who knew no fear ;

Those killed in the Cause of God yet live and thrive and do rejoice ;

And never can those who fight against Faith hurt in the least the Cause of God.

60. Regard, unmoved, the taunts of those who laugh at faith ; nor let their falsehood nor their seeming prosperity, raise questions in your minds.

All who can read the Signs of God in Nature know His wisdom, goodness, power, and justice.

They know His promise is sure, and, in humble prayer, wholly put their trust in Him.

WHAT IS A GOOD LIFE IN SOCIETY?

S. 4. 61. All mankind are one, and mutual rights must be respected :

The sexes must honour, each the other ;

Sacred are family relationships that rise through marriage and women bearing children ;

Orphans need especial loving care ;

In trust is held all property, with duties well-defined ;

And after death, due distribution should be made in equitable shares to all whose affection, duty, and trust shed light and joy on this our life below.

62. What can be a holier cement to Society than that women and men should be chaste and pure, and crimes against sex rooted out ?

Let decency, kindness, and justice prevail in all sex relationships ;

Let marriage be cherished and carefully guarded ; women's rights secured ; family jars adjusted ; and all life lived in faith, charity, and kindness sincere to all our fellow-creatures.

63. Be clean and pure, and seek no occasions for quibbles, nor go after sorcery or false gods.

Be faithful in your trusts, learn obedience, and settle your quarrels under the guidance of God's Apostle.

Ever keep away from hypocrisy and every kind of falsehood.

Then will you be admitted to a glorious Fellowship with the highest and noblest in the spiritual world.

64. Keep together in your noble Brotherhood :

Share its joys and sorrows : strive and fight the good fight and fear not : for this life is short, and the Hereafter eternal.

Allow not yourselves to be drawn into unbelief and cowardice : maintain the Right.

Protect yourselves against Hypocrites and Deserters, but pursue them not unrelentingly.

65. The lives of those who believe are sacred :

If one is slain by mistake, full compensation should be made.

Nor should a stranger, even in time of war, be treated as an enemy, without the fullest investigation.

Live not in places hostile to Islam, if ye are able to migrate, and spacious is God's earth.

Devotion and prayer may be shortened in times of danger.

Take every precaution for safety, but be bold and undaunted in fight.

66. Beware of treachery, that would use the good and pious for its wicked ends :

Its plots will but recoil on its own head.

The righteous have no cause for secrecy, except in doing good.

'Tis evil that misleads, deceives, and even dares deface fair Nature, as by God created.

Shun all evil, and be firm in righteousness and faith in God.

67. Justice to women and orphans is part of religion and the fear of God.

Stand out firmly for justice to all, even against yourselves or your nearest of kin.

Remain firm in faith, and consort not with evil or hypocrisy.

Be true in speech, and wound not others :

Nor distinguish between Teachers of Truth, for God's Truth is one and should be believed.

68. The People of the Book went wrong : the Jews in breaking their Covenant, and slandering Mary and Jesus, and in their usury and injustice ; and the Christians in raising Jesus the Apostle to equality with God.

God's revelation is continued in the Qur-ān, which comes with manifest proof and a clear light to those who understand.

DEPARTURE FROM FAITH, JUSTICE, AND DUTY; AND THEIR CONSEQUENCES

S. 5. 69. All obligations are sacred, human or divine.

In the spiritual world we owe duties to God, which must be fulfilled.

But whilst we are in this world of sense, those duties are by no means isolated from what we owe to ourselves and our fellows in the world of men.

We must respect the laws and customs of the Sacred Mosque and the Sacred Sanctuary.

In food our laws are simple : all things good and pure are lawful.

We refuse not social intercourse with men and women,— people of the Book.

70. God wishes us to be clean and pure, at prayer and at other times.

But justice and right conduct even in the face of spite and hatred, are nearest to Piety and the love of God :

In Him we put our trust.

71. If men who received revelations before were false to their trust, if they broke their agreements and twisted God's Message from its aim, if they rebelled against Truth and followed their fancies, God's grace was withdrawn from them and they wandered in the wilderness.

72. The jealousy of Cain against Abel, which led to the murder of innocent Abel, is the type of the jealousy between the People of the Book and their younger brethren in Islam.

Jealousy leads to envy and murder.

Such crimes against individuals are often crimes against whole peoples.

There are men who are ready to catch up every lie told against a just man. The just man should not grieve, for that is their way.

73. True justice accords with God's Law.

Follow not men's selfish desires, but God's Will, which was revealed to Moses and Jesus, and now to Muḥammad.

Take not for friends and protectors those in whose hearts is a disease,—to whom religion is a mockery or a plaything, —who worship evil.

Proclaim the Truth of God, and be not afraid.

Eschew their iniquities, which were denounced by David and Jesus.

But recognise with justice those who are sincere and humble, though they may be themselves not of your flock, if they witness to Truth.

74. In the physical pleasures of life the crime is excess : there is no merit in abstention from things that are good and lawful.

Take no rash vows, but to solemn oaths be faithful.

Shun as abominations drinking and gambling and superstition of all kinds,

But be reverent to what is sacred in rites and associations.

Not the same are things good and things evil.

Learn to distinguish, but pry not into questions beyond your ken.

Guard your own souls in truth and justice, and no harm can befall you.

75. Jesus did feed his disciples by miracle, but he claimed not divinity :

He was a true servant of God, to Whom doth belong the dominion of the heavens and the earth :

Glory and power are His, and His alone.

GOD AND THE HEREAFTER

S. 6. 76. God did separate Light from Darkness ; He reigns not only in heaven but also on earth ; Mercy is His Law ; to Him shall we all return at the end of all things.

How can we then depart from truth and forge lies against Him ?

It is folly to say that there is nothing beyond this our present life.

77. The life of this world is but empty : what is serious is the life hereafter.

The teacher of God's truth is not baulked by frivolous objections or insults or persecution.

The wicked will be cut off to the last remnant.

God's wisdom pervades the whole of His Creation, and in His hands are the keys of the Unseen, and the secrets of all that we see.

78. God's loving care doth encompass us round throughout life, and deliver us from dangers by land and sea.

He is the only Protector : how can we then forget Him or run after things that are mere creatures of His, and shall perish,—while He is the Eternal God, adored by Abraham and all the prophets?

79. The good men and true, who succeeded Abraham, received the gifts of revelation and guidance, and kept alive God's Message,

Which now is proclaimed in the Qur-ān, in which is blessing and confirmation of all that went before.

In the daily pageants of Nature,—the dawn and the restful night, the sun, the moon, the stars that guide the mariner in distant seas, the rain-clouds pouring abundance, and the fruits that delight the heart of man—can ye not read Signs of God?

No vision can comprehend Him, yet He knoweth and comprehendeth all.

80. Those in obstinate rebellion against God are merely deceived and deceive each other.

Leave them alone, but trust and obey God openly and in the inmost recesses of your heart.

The plans of the wicked are but plans against their own souls.

81. God punishes not mere shortcoming:

There are degrees in good and evil deeds.

God is Merciful, but His Plan is sure, and none can stand in its way.

We must avoid all superstition and all excess, and humbly ask for His guidance.

82. God's commands are not irrational taboos, but based on the moral law, and conformable to reason.

His Way is the straight Way, of justice and truth.

In unity and faith must we dedicate all our life to His service, and His alone, to Whom we shall return.

REVELATION: A MERCY AND GUIDANCE

S. 7. 83. Revelation should ease the difficulties of heart and mind,

For it tells the story of man's spiritual past, and teaches the end of good and evil.

Iblīs fell from jealousy and arrogance, and Adam fell because he listened to his deceit.

But God did grant in His Mercy gifts and guidance to men, warned them against excess, and taught them moderation and justice.

84. God has forbidden the things that are evil, not those that are good, for these were created for man's enjoyment.

The transgressors are those who reject God's Signs.

They will have no share in the Bliss of the Hereafter.

But the righteous will dwell in Peace, and the Hope that was promised will be theirs.

85. Noah's warning was rejected by his generation, and they were destroyed in the Flood.

Hūd was defied by his own people 'Ād, but they were swept away by a terrible blast.

Their successors, the Thamūd, were puffed up with pride and injustice, but behold ! an earthquake buried them for their sins after Ṣāliḥ had warned them from God.

With a rain of brimstone and fire were overwhelmed the

Cities of the Plain for their unexampled lusts, against which Lot did warn them.

The people of Midian were given to mischief and fraud : Shu'aib did warn them, but they heeded not, and perished in an earthquake.

God's punishment is sure for wickedness and sin.

86. While the story of the prophets who preached in vain to their people pre-figures the struggles in the early careers of all apostles,

The story of Moses,—his struggles with an alien and arrogant people, his final deliverance of his people from foreign domination, and his leading them within sight of the Promised Land, in spite of the forces that resisted,—pre-figures the early struggles and eventual triumph of Muḥammad the Holy Apostle of God.

87. With the advent of the Holy Apostle, the light and guidance which he brought for all mankind from God superseded the earlier Law for the Jews.

The good and the upright among them followed the new Light, but the rest were scattered through the earth.

88. Mankind have the nature of good created within them : Yet doth God by His Signs keep up a constant reminder to men, of His holy Names.

Those who err scarce realise how gradually they fall into sin.

Their respite has a term ; the doom must come, and it may be on a sudden.

So humbly draw nigh to the Lord, declare His glory, and rejoice in His service.

S. 8. 89. Fight the good fight, but dispute not about the prize : that is for God to give.

Men of faith act and obey.

'Tis nobler to fight for Truth than to seek worldly gain.

To the pure in faith God will give the mind and the resources to conquer.

They but fight, with no thought of ever turning back : the victory should be ascribed to God, not men.

90. Be ready to obey God's call, and to hold all else as naught : He will give you the light, turn away all evil from you, and forgive you your sins and shortcomings.

Ever keep in remembrance His mercies and grace.

The godless may try to keep men from God, but they will not thrive : they will be hurled together to destruction.

91. The battle of Badr brought to an issue the fight between Truth and Unbelief.

It was the Day of Differentiation.

Not for spoils was it won, nor by numbers ;

But by courage and planning, union of wills, and pooling of strength and resources,—

Above all by the help of God, Whose help is ever all-sufficient.

92. No man of heart, spirit, or constancy can ever be cowed down by odds against him.

We fight not for spoils or for captives, but for the glory of God, and for truth and faith.

We must be kind to all, but specially regard the needs of our comrades, linked to us by ties of duty and affection.

Our highest reward will be forgiveness and grace from the Giver of all.

IN FACE OF HOSTILITY AND TREACHERY

S. 9.   93. If the Pagans repeatedly break their treaties, denounce the treaties,

But give them time either to repent or to prepare for the just punishment of their treachery.

Punish the chiefs of the treacherous, and destroy them.

But if one of them seeks asylum, give it : let him hear the Word of God and escort him to security.

Be true to the true, but fight those who are false to plighted word and taunt you for your Faith.

(*Note to S. 8.*   The little exiled community of Mecca Muslims, with their friends in Medina, had organised themselves into a God-fearing community, but were constantly in danger of being attacked by their Pagan enemies of Mecca, in alliance with some of the disaffected elements (Jews and Hypocrites) in or near Medina itself. The design of the Meccans was to gather all the resources they could, and with an overwhelming force, to crush and annihilate Muḥammad and his party. To this end Abū Sufyān was leading a richly-laden caravan from Syria to Mecca. He called for armed aid from Mecca. The battle was fought in the plain of Badr, about 50 miles south-west of Medina. The Muslim force consisted of only about 313 men, mostly unarmed, but they were led by Muḥammad, and they were fighting for their Faith. The Meccan army, well-armed and well-equipped, numbered over a thousand, and had among its leaders some of the most experienced warriors of Arabia, including Abū Jahl, the inveterate foe and persecutor of Islam. Against all odds the Muslims won a brilliant victory.)

No one has the right to approach the mosques of God unless he believes in God and follows God's Law, the law of righteousness.

94. The enemies of Faith would fain put out God's light, but God's light will shine more glorious than ever.

Wealth is for use and on trust for mankind : hoard not, nor misuse it.

Fight a straight fight in the cause of Right :

Go forth bravely to strive and struggle, and prove yourselves worthy of God.

95. The Believers do their duty, and make no excuses,—unlike the Hypocrites, who are a burden whether they join you or hold back.

No help should be accepted from these last, as they are false and insincere, and have a slanderous tongue.

Alms are for the poor and the needy, not for those who come in hypocrisy and mock at things solemn.

But the hypocrites will be found out and receive due punishment, while the righteous will be rewarded with bliss and the good pleasure of God.

96. The hardest striving and fighting are needed to combat evil and hypocrisy ;

For sin can reach a stage when the doors of forgiveness are closed.

The good must shun all evil as unclean, and gladly welcome all chance of service and sacrifice, as bringing them closer to the Presence and Mercy of God.

97. The vanguard of Faith think nothing of self-sacrifice. Their reward is God's Good Pleasure.

Even those who do wrong but repent will obtain His Mercy:

Not so those who persist in Unfaith, Hypocrisy, and Mischief.

God's grace is free and abounding for the righteous. Even if they waver or fail, He will turn to them in Mercy, if only they repent and come back unto Him.

98. To be true in word and deed is to hold our selfish desires at bay, and follow God's Call:

In this is our fullest satisfaction and reward.

But our striving should include study and teaching, for the Brethren's benefit.

For God's Message increases our Faith and leads us to love Him and trust Him, the Lord of the Throne of Glory Supreme.

GOD IS GOOD

S. 10. 99. Men may wonder that a man like unto them should bring a Message from God, but God's Message shines forth through all nature and Creation.

He guides the human spirit, if only man will have Faith and put his hope in God.

Wonderful are God's relations with man, yet man is ungrateful and runs to fancies and fanciful gods.

Glory to the One true God, Who made mankind as one,
And holds alone the secrets of the Unseen in His great and good Universal Plan.

100. The good, the beautiful, and the useful in man's life are derived from God; yet man is ungrateful.

He runs after the ephemeral things of this life;

Yet they are no better than the green of the fields, that lasts for a season ere it perish!

God's call is to an eternal Home of Peace.

Will ye not answer it?

Know ye not that it is He Who sustains and cherishes?

No partner has He.

And He speaks to His creatures and guides them through His wonderful Book unmatched.

101. Men but wrong their own souls in shutting out the Truth of God.

To Him will be their return.

They have been warned at all times and among all peoples by chosen Apostles of God, whom they have flouted.

The Day will come when they will see the majesty, the glory, the goodness, and the justice of God.

But they invent fancies and falsehoods.

Let not their blasphemies and falsehoods grieve the men of God: for falsehoods and false ones will never prosper.

102. God works in His world—in mercy for His servants, and in just punishment for those who do wrong.

Thus was it in Noah's story, for he worked unselfishly for his people, though rejected of them.

So was it with Moses: he preached to Pharaoh and the Egyptians, but most of them preferred falsehood and pride to the Truth of God, and perished.

Even Pharaoh's confession of God at the last was too late, as his life had been spent in luxury, pride, and oppression.

103. God's purpose of Mercy and Forgiveness was shown in the mission of Jonah,

When Nineveh was pardoned on repentance, and given a new lease of life.

We must be patient and strive with constancy and perseverance,

For all suffering and sorrow as well as all bounties proceed from God,

Whose plan is righteous and for the good of His creatures.

MAN IS UNGRATEFUL

S. 11. 104. God's Revelation teaches the Truth : it warns against wrong and gives glad tidings to the righteous :

Ungrateful man folds up his heart and fails to see how all Nature points to God and to the Hereafter :

He but seeks petty issues, forgetting the Cause of Causes.

Not all the wisdom of man can produce aught like the Message which comes from God, as the Light that leads and the Mercy that forgives.

Who then but will humble himself before God, seeking His light and His voice ?

105. Noah walked righteously and humbly as in the sight of God.

With unselfish love for his people he warned them and taught them.

But they did flout and reject his Message with scorn and insults.

God gave him directions to build an Ark against the impending Flood which was to purify the world from Sin and Unrighteousness.

In it were saved Noah and those who believed.

So were promised salvation and God's Peace and Blessings to the Righteous evermore !

106. Awful were the fates of the 'Ād and the Thamūd, two mighty peoples of ancient Arabia.

They rejected God and His Message and went on in their evil ways,—

The 'Ād in their superstitions and arrogance, and the Thamūd in their entrenched selfishness, denying to others the gifts of God's spacious earth !

How swiftly were they wiped out, as if they had never been ?

But wrong can never stand !

107. When the angels, on a mission to Sodom and Gomorrah, Cities of the Plain, passed by Abraham,

He entertained them and received from them the Good News of the line of Prophets to spring from his loins.

He tried, in his goodness of heart, to intercede for the wicked Cities, but they were steeped in sin and past all hope of repentance.

Lot preached to them, but they flouted him and went to their fate, as also did Midian.

The People of Shu'aib destroyed their commerce by fraudulent dealings and love of brute force.

Marvellous are God's Mercies, and strange are the ways
of ungrateful man !

108. How the arrogant Pharaoh misled his people in
resisting God's Message through Moses !

Thus did they ruin themselves !

It was they who wronged themselves : for God is ever
kind and His punishments are just.

All men will be brought to His Judgment-seat, and the
good will be rewarded with bliss, as the evil will be consigned
to misery.

Eschew evil ; stand firm in righteousness ; be not im-
mersed in the lusts of this world.

Learn from the stories of the past, and seek the Lord's
Mercy : trust Him and serve and praise Him for ever !

THE STORY OF JOSEPH

S. 12. 109. Life and Wisdom are explained by Signs, Symbols,
Parables, and moving Stories, in the Holy Qur-ān.

A beautiful story is that of Joseph, the best-beloved son
of Jacob.

His future greatness was pre-figured in a vision, but his
brothers were filled with envy and hate :

They plotted to get rid of him and threw him down into
a well.

Some merchants found him, bound for Egypt.

The brothers sold him into slavery for a few silver coins,—

Him the noblest man of his age, marked out by God for a
destiny of greatness, righteousness, and benevolence.

110. Joseph was bought by a man high at Court in Egypt,

Who asked his wife (Zulaik͟hā) to treat him with honour, with a view to his adoption as a son.

But she burnt with passion of earthly love for him.

When Joseph refused to yield to her solicitations, there was trouble and scandal, and Joseph was imprisoned.

Here were shown his greatness, and kindness, and wisdom.

The King's cup-bearer came in disgrace to prison.

Joseph instructed him and others in the eternal Gospel of Unity.

When released and restored to favour, the cup-bearer forgot Joseph—for a time,—

Until it pleased God to put into Joseph's hands the keys of the prosperity of Egypt and the world.

111. The king of Egypt saw a vision which none of his grandees could explain.

The cup-bearer referred to Joseph, who was sent for by the king.

But Joseph insisted that the voice of scandal, which had pointed to him, should be declared in public to be false.

After Zulaik͟hā had paid a splendid ungrudging tribute to his truth and righteousness, he came, and was invested with supreme power by the king.

In times of plenty he organised great reserves to meet the needs of famine.

When wide-spread famine at last prevailed, his brothers came from Canaan in search of corn.

He treated them kindly and got them to bring his youngest brother Benjamin : but they knew not he was Joseph.

112. When the brothers went back without Benjamin, Jacob was overwhelmed with grief,

But he bore his affliction with patience and faith in God.

He refused to be comforted and sent his sons back, to Egypt.

At last Joseph revealed himself, forgave them, and sent his shirt by them to Jacob, to tell him the good news that Joseph lived and did great work in Egypt,

And had sent for his whole family to come and rejoice and live in the land of Egypt, and be a blessing to all.

113. Jacob was comforted with the news.

The whole family moved to Egypt, where Joseph received them with honour.

He forgave his brothers, thanked and praised God, and lived and died a righteous man.

So the story shows how the Plan of God doth work without fail :

It defeats the wiles of the wicked, turns evil to good, and ever leads those who are true to beatitudes undreamt of.

So did it happen in Mustafā's life.

Will man not learn to rely on God as the only Reality, turning away from all that is fleeting or untrue ?

GOD'S REVELATION: HOW IT WORKS

S. 13.   114. God's Truth comes to man in revelation and in nature.

How noble are His works ! How sublime His government of the world ! They all declare forth His glory !

Yet man must strangely resist Faith, and ask to see the Signs of His power rather than the Signs of His Mercy !

Doth not His knowledge search through the most hidden things ?

Are not Lightning and Thunder the Signs of His Might as well as of His Mercy ?

He alone is worthy of praise, and His Truth will stand when all vanities pass away like scum on the torrent of Time.

115. The seeing and the blind are not alike : nor are those blessed with Faith and those without.

The former seek God, and attain peace and blessedness in their hearts, and a final Home of rest.

The latter are in a state of Curse, and their End is terrible.

If God in His wisdom postpones retribution, it is for a time.

His promise never fails : it will come to pass in His own good time.

In all things it is for Him to command.

116. The mockery of God's apostles is an old game of the world.

But God's Truth will come to its own in good time.

The End of the righteous is their Home of Bliss, and they rejoice in the revelations they receive.

The Messengers of God take their due share in the life of the world ; they win through by God's grace against all the plots of the world.

Their witness is from God, through His revelation.

S. 14. 117. Revelation leads mankind from the depths of darkness into light.

It comes to every age and nation in its own language.

So was it before ; so will it be always.

The apostles were doubted, insulted, threatened, and persecuted, but their trust was sure in God.

It is Evil that will be wiped out.

God's Truth is as a goodly tree, firmly established on its roots, stretching its branches high and wide, and bearing good fruit at all times.

118. But the evil not only choose evil for themselves but mislead others to perdition.

The godly should learn from the Signs of God all around them, and be on their guard against all that is false.

So Abraham prayed not only for his posterity, but for all :

For he foresaw the universality of God's Message in Islam.

That leads to the mystic doctrine of Oneness,

Which will be seen in its fulness on the Great Day when a new Earth and a new Heaven will proclaim the end of Evil and the adjustment of all this life's accounts.

S. 15. 119. God's Truth makes all things clear, and He will guard it.

But His Signs are not for those who mock.

Who fails to see the majesty, beauty, order, and harmony blazoned in His Creation,

And His goodness to all His creatures, in the heavens and on earth ?

With Him are the sources of all things, and He doth freely give his gifts in due measure.

He holds The keys of Life and Death, and He will remain when all else passes away.

120. Man's origin was from dust, lowly ;
But his rank was raised above that of other creatures because God breathed into him His spirit.

Jealousy and arrogance caused the fall of Iblis, the Power of Evil :
But no power has Evil o'er those sincere souls who worship God and seek His Way.

Many are the gates of Evil, but Peace and dignified joy will be the goal of those whom the Grace of God has made His own.

121. God's Grace and Mercy are always first, but His Justice and Wrath will seize those who defy His Law.

Even when the unspeakable crimes of the Cities of the Plain made their destruction inevitable, God's message of Mercy to mankind was sent to Abraham and of safety to Lot.

The last remnants of Sin will be cut off, and the Signs and Tokens thereof are plain for all to see.

The proud Companions of the Wood and the builders of Rocky Fortresses were all swept away because of their sins.

122. But God's Creation doth bear witness to God's Design and Mercy.

His Plan is sure.

His gift of the glorious Qur-ān is more than any worldly goods can be.

So, while we denounce Sin openly, let us be gentle and kind, and adore and serve our Lord all our lives.

S. 16.   123.   God's Command must inevitably come to pass.

But all His Creation proclaims His glory, and leads to His Truth.

In all things has He furnished man with favours innumerable, to lead and guide him and bring him to Himself.

Why then does man refuse the Truth, except for arrogance ?

Why does he run after false gods, thus acting against his own lights and misleading others less blest in knowledge ?

124.   In all ages wicked men tried to plot against God's Way, but they never succeeded, and were covered with shame in ways unexpected.

The righteous see good in God's Word, and their goal is the Good.

Great Teachers were sent to all nations, to warn against Evil and guide to the Right.

The penalty for evil comes in many unexpected ways, for Evil is against Nature.

And all Nature proclaims God's Glory and humbly serves Him, the Lord Supreme.

125.   There is but One God, He Who gives all blessings to man and other creatures.

His greatest gift is that He reveals Himself.

But in many tangible ways he cares for man and provides for his growth and sustenance.

In rain, in milk, in fruits and honey, and in Nature and the life of man, with his opportunities of social, moral, and spiritual growth, are Signs for those who understand.

Why then does man show ingratitude by going after false gods and forgetting God ?

126. God's apostles, if rejected, will be witnesses against those who reject God's Truth !

And all false gods will disappear.

A life of justice and righteousness is enjoined by God, and the strictest fidelity, in intent and action.

For God will judge us by our faith and deeds, and no evil shall have power over those who believe and put their trust in God their Lord.

127. God's Truth may come in stages, but it gives strength, guidance, and glad tidings, and should be held fast when once received.

Be not like those who get puffed up with pride in worldly good, and scorn the Truth.

Enjoy the good things of life, but render thanks to God and obey His Law.

Be true in faith, and proclaim His Word with gentle, patient wisdom :

For God is with those who live in self-restraint a pure, and righteous life.

RESPONSIBILITY OF EACH INDIVIDUAL LIFE

S. 17. 128. It is the privilege of the men of God to see the sublimest mysteries of the spiritual world and instruct men in Righteousness ;

They warn and shield men against Evil.

But nothing can lessen each soul's personal responsibility for its own deeds.

It carries its fate round its own neck.

God's gifts are for all, but not all receive the same gifts, nor are all gifts of equal dignity or excellence.

129. To be worthy of the service of the One True God, we must love and serve His Creatures.

The parents who cherished us in childhood deserve our humble reverence and service :

Next come the rights of kinsmen, those in want, and way-faring strangers :

To each according to his need, not in spendrift show.

And gentleness is needed to those whom we cannot help.

God will provide. He has made life sacred and pure.

Fulfil your trusts for orphans and deal with all in strictest probity.

Pry not into evil from curiosity, and shun insolence : for God hates evil,—

The One, the Good, the Universal Lord !

130. There is none like unto God. Exalted beyond measure is He.

All Creation declares His glory.

His revelation is Truth, but is beyond comprehension to those who believe not in the Hereafter.

Those who serve Him should beware lest words unseemly should escape them, whether to friend or foe.

Avoid dissensions, and know that God's Wrath when kindled is a terrible thing ;

But we rejoice that He forbears and forgives.

131. Arrogance, jealousy, spite, and hatred were the cause of the fall of Iblis.

Man was given pre-eminence above much of God's Creation, and owes higher responsibilities.

He should give thanks for God's mercies, and remember the Day of Account.

Not all the scheming of Evil will deflect God's righteous Plan to protect His chosen ones.

They should pray without ceasing, and seek His true Guidance ;

For Truth will last, but Falsehood will perish.

132. Who can define the Spirit of Inspiration ?

Its gift is the highest of God's Mercies to man.

The Qur-ān is divine, and no carpings can affect its greatness or the greatness of the Messenger who brought it to men.

Those who reject it will be called to account on the Day of Judgment.

Let not Pride and Ignorance rush, like Pharaoh, to the Punishment of the Hereafter.

The Qur-ān as revealed by stages teaches the Truth :

Learn it and chant it, and praise the Beautiful Names of God for ever !

S. 18.   133. The Book of Revelation gives straight directions to make our lives straight,—

To warn us against Evil and guide us to the Good everlasting.

Teach the Truth, but fret not about men rejecting it.

The Parable of the Companions of the Cave shows how God works wonders beyond our fathoming :

How Faith is a sure refuge in ways we know not ;

How Time itself works God's Plan before we know how it passes ;

How He can give us rest, and raise us back to life against all odds ;

And how futile it is to engage in controversies about matters we know not.

134. True knowledge is with God alone.

We are not to dispute on matters of conjecture, but to rely on the Truth that comes from God.

As in the Parable, the man who piles up wealth and is puffed up with this world's goods, despising those otherwise endowed, will come to an evil end, for his hopes were not built on God.

135. The life of this world is ephemeral, and its gains will not last.

Good Deeds are the best of possessions in God's sight :

All will be levelled up on the Day of Judgment, and a new Order created on the basis of Truth, according to the Book of Deeds.

Pride is the root of Evil, rebellion, and wrong.

Who will choose evil ones in preference to God ?

Let us accept Truth, for though Falsehood may flourish for a time, it must perish in the end.

136. Moses was up against mysteries which he wanted to explore.

He searched out a man endued with knowledge derived from the divine springs from which flow the paradoxes of life.

He is shown three such paradoxes and how human impatience is inconsistent with their true understanding.

The highest knowledge comes not except by divine gift,
And a constant, patient striving, with Faith, to apprehend
something of the purpose of the All-wise God.

137. Three episodes in the life of a great King, Zul-qarnain, illustrate how power and opportunities should be used in the service of God :
He punished the guilty indeed, but was kind to the righteous;
He left primitive people their freedom of life ;
And he protected industrious people from grasping neighbours.
But he relied upon God, and made them remember the Day of Judgment,
When all will see the Truth and receive the Punishments and Rewards earned in their present life.

S. 19. 138. Men of God show their qualities in their private relationships as much as in their public ministry.
Zakariyā was anxious, in a world of unrighteousness, to find a successor to continue his godly errand.
He was given a son, Yahyā, who heralded Jesus, and lived a life of wisdom, gentle love, and purity.

139. Next comes the story of Jesus and his mother Mary.
She gave birth, as a virgin, to Jesus, but her people slandered and abused her as a disgrace to her lineage.
Her son did defend her and was kind to her.
He was a servant of God, a true Prophet, blessed in the gifts of Prayer and Charity, but no more than a man :

To call him the son of God is to derogate from God's Majesty, for God is High above all His Creatures, the Judge of the Last Day.

140. Abraham pleaded with loving earnestness with his father to accept the truth of God :

He was turned out, but he retained His gentleness and was blessed.

Moses asked for the aid of his brother Aaron and was true to his people.

Ismā'īl was loyal to his father and his God, and was a willing and accepted sacrifice to God.

141. Why should man disbelieve in the Hereafter ?

We all must pass through the fire of temptation, but God Most Gracious will save us if we accept Him and do right.

Sin may have its respite, but must run to its own destruction.

We must not dishonour God by holding false and monstrous ideas of Him.

Glory to Him that He cares for all His creatures !

S. 20.   142. God's revelation is not an occasion for man's distress :

It is a Message to show that God All-Knowing sits on the throne of Mercy and guides all affairs.

There is no god but He ; to Him belong all the most beautiful Names.

143. The story of how Moses was chosen and told of his mission, has a high mystic meaning.

He was true to his family and solicitous for their welfare.

Encamped in the desert, he saw a fire far off.

Approaching, he found it was holy ground.

God did reveal Himself to him, so that he saw life in things lifeless, and light in his glorified Hand, that shone white with light divine.

Armed with these Signs he was told to go forth on his mission.

But he thought of his brother Aaron, and prayed that God might join him in his mission, and his prayer was granted.

144. From his birth was Moses prepared for his task.

His mother received guidance, so that God's purpose might be fulfilled.

Moses was brought up in Pharaoh's palace and trained in all the learning of Egypt.

Yet he drank the love of his people in his mother's milk.

Adventures and trials he had, including his stay with the Midianites—until he was called to his double mission :

To preach to Pharaoh and the Egyptians, and to free his own people.

So he and Aaron went to Pharaoh, who rejected God and His Signs, but appointed a trial of strength between his magicians and Moses.

Moses won ; and the Truth of God was accepted by some Egyptians, but not by Pharaoh.

145. The people of Israel were rescued from bondage and led on their way to the Promised Land.

God's Grace gave them light and guidance, but they rebelled under the leadership of one called the Sāmirī :

He melted the gold of their jewels and made an idol—a calf—for their worship—a thing without life or power.

Moses destroyed the idol, and cursed the man who led the people astray.

146. Such is the lure of Evil;

But high and low will be levelled on the Day of Judgment, before the Eternal, the Gracious, the King, the Truth, who sends the Qur-ān to teach and to warn.

Will man remember how Adam's arch-enemy, Satan, caused his fall, and will he yet be blind to the Signs of God?

Nay,—but let not Evil make you impatient:

The Prize of the Hereafter is better than aught of the glitter of this life:

Wait in Faith, and the End will show the triumph of Truth, Goodness, and Righteousness.

S. 21. 147. Men may lightly treat God's Signs as jests, but the Judgment must come inevitably.

His Message is true, and delivered by God's Apostle, as from man to men.

Truth must triumph, and all false gods and false worship must come to naught:

For God is One, and His Truth has been one throughout the ages.

148. Look at God's Creation: contemplate its unity of Design and benevolence of Purpose.

Death must come to all, but life and faith are not objects of ridicule.

Truth will outlast all mockery:

'Tis God who calls, because He cares for you, and on His Judgment-Seat will weigh each act, each thought, each motive, great or small, with perfect justice.

Come, ye all, reject not His blessed Message.

149. The great exemplars of virtue conquered Evil, each according to his circumstances :

Abraham stood staunch in the fire of persecution, unhurt ;

Lot was bold in reproving abominations ;

Noah survived the Flood by his faith, in a world of Unbelief ;

David sought justice, and sang God's praises ;

Solomon by wisdom subdued the refractory ;

Job was patient in suffering ; Ismā'īl, Idrīs, and Zul-kifl were true in constancy amid temptation ;

Jonah turned to God after a short misunderstanding ;

Zakarīyā and his family were exemplars of devoutness ; and Mary of chastity.

All men and women of God form one united Brotherhood.

150. No good deed is fruitless :

Work while yet there's time : for with Judgment the door will be closed to repentance.

No false gods of fancy can help.

The Righteous will have no fear ;

For them the angelic greetings will truly open a new world, which they will inherit.

This was God's Message of old, and the same is God's Message renewed :

For God is one, and so is His Message proclaimed for all, freely and in loving Truth.

S. 22. 151. Will not mankind take warning from the dreadful consequences of Evil clearly proclaimed to them?

Will they dispute about God and the Life of the Future?

They have only to look around and within them, and they will see vestiges of the Plan and Purpose of God.

Let them not halt between Good and Evil: God's Message as well as His Messenger must win against all obstacles.

Only the evil will be brought to shame and agony.

The good—whose speech is pure and conduct worthy of praise—will have a meed of refinement, beauty, and bliss.

152. For our spiritual growth are provided symbols and means of expression in our ordinary lives.

Such is the Pilgrimage, meant to gather men and women from far and near to share in sacrifice, and prayer and praise, in an age-old centre of worship.

The sacrifices, too, are symbols of Piety of Heart, a longing to share with fellow-men in the bounties of God.

In the Fight for Truth is tested our purity of motive, unselfishness of aim, and devotion to Right at the cost of self.

Fearless must we fight; for Truth has often been flouted, but must finally win.

153. The power of Evil is in insidious suggestions:

They are only a trial to those whose hearts are inclined to evil.

But Truth doth shine the nobler for the Believers, by the grace and guidance of God.

Martyrs who give their all in the cause of God will find
a provision ample and eternal.

The finest and subtlest mysteries are but proofs of the
goodness of God.

Dispute not about rites and ceremonies : follow the
Straight Way.

Seek for worship the Only True God, and strive in His
service,

That ye may be witnesses among men to God's Truth, as
the Apostle is a witness to you.

S. 23. 154. Faith leads to humility, avoidance of vanity in word
and deed, charity, continence, faithful observance of trusts
and covenants, and devout approach to God—surest steps
to Bliss.

Man carries in himself proofs of God's Providence ;

The same story is told if he looks at nature around him ;

And the long line of Teachers sent by God shows God's
special care of humanity.

What though they were rejected and scorned, maligned and
persecuted ?

God's Truth won through, as it always will.

155. The Brotherhood of Truth is one in all ages : it is
the narrow men who create sects.

Let them not think that the goods of this world can shield
them from evil or its consequences.

God's Truth and His Messenger can be known to all :

For He in His Mercy has given us faculties and judgment,
if we would but use them.

The Message is not new : all Creation proclaims it : High above all is the Lord of Glory Supreme !

156. Let us eschew evil, but not pay back evil in its own coin, however great the temptation :

No chance will there be to retrieve our conduct, once death cuts us off.

Then we shall only have to wait for Judgment :

None can miss that Barrier :

Our deeds will be weighed, and happy those whose good weighs more in the scale than ill.

Only Faith and Goodness will prevail in the end :

So glory to the Lord of the Throne exalted, of Mercy and Honour !

S. 24. 157. Chastity is a virtue, for men and women, whether joined in marriage, or single or widowed.

The punishment for offences in such matters should be public.

No less grave is the launching of false charges or rumours against the fair reputation of women, or the spreading of such slanders, or the facile belief in them.

Evil is ever spreading its net.

Good men and women should ever be on their guard, and pray for God's grace and mercy.

158. Privacy in the home is a nurse of virtue : respect it with dignity.

Guard your eyes and thoughts with rules of modesty in dress and manners :

And learn from these to keep your spiritual gaze from straying to any but God.

True marriage should teach us chastity and purity,

And such are the virtues which lead us to the Light sublime which illuminates the world.

159. God is the Light of the heavens and the earth.

High above our petty evanescent lives, He illumines our souls with means that reach our inmost being.

Universal is His light, so pure and so intense that grosser beings need a veil to take His rays :

His elect are e'er absorbed in prayer and praise and deeds of love,

Unlike the children of Darkness, struggling in depths profound of vanities false.

All Nature sings to the glory of God,

And men of fraud and hypocrisy are but rebels in the Kingdom of God.

160. For a self-respecting life on earth, respect for others' privacy is most essential, in the home and abroad :

But superstitions are not meet in intercourse amongst kin or true friends.

In public council never fail to observe the most punctilious form and order :

Your self-respect demands that ye should give your Leader sincere respect and all obedience.

Ye may not know but God doth know the inwardness of things both great and small.

S. 25. 161. Among the highest and greatest of the gifts of God is His Revelation,

Which is the Criterion by which we may judge between right and wrong—

Between false and true worship, between the Message that comes from God and the forgeries of men, between the Real in our eternal Future and the Fancies by which we are misled.

The apostles of God come as men to live among men and guide them.

162. Woe to the misbelievers who arrogantly demand to see God, yet reject His Signs!

The Judgment will come, and then they will see, too late, how evil casts nothing but treacherous snares for man.

Slowly comes God's Revelation, in ways most conducive to man's enlightenment.

Men in their folly reject the most obvious Signs of God.

Let them mock! Soon will they know!

Alas! men ruled by self-impulse are worse than brute beasts to guide or control!

163. But the Signs of God are everywhere in creation.

The Sun and the Shadow, the Day and the Night, the Wind and the Rain,—all things in nature are symbols, and point to the Law Divine, and the destiny, good or ill, of man.

Will he not learn and put his trust in Him, the Merciful?

His true servants ever adore him in humility and fear of wrong,

In faith and just moderation in life,

In respect for duties owed to God and men and self,

In avoidance of all that is false or futile,

In strict and grateful attention to God's Message,

And in the wish to put themselves and their families in the van of those who love and honour God.

S. 26. 164. God's plan works unceasingly : His Light shines none the less brightly, because some reject it or mock at it.

Moses was freed from all fear when God gave him His Signs and sent him to Pharaoh :

He boldly proclaimed the Message, and won the wise ones of Egypt :

The rejecters, with Pharaoh, perished, and their heritage passed to worthier hands.

165. Abraham patiently argued with his people about God's Truth ;

Prayed for wisdom and righteousness, for himself, his father, and future generations ; and taught Truth about the Hereafter.

Noah preached to a world of Unfaith, and would not reject the humble and lowly :

His arrogant rejecters were brought low : in him and his following were vindicated God's righteous Purpose and Mercy.

166. The 'Ād were addicted to arrogance ; they exulted in material strength and possessions, and had no faith but in force :

They were brought low, as were the Thamūd, who gave way to extravagance, and were guilty of sacrilege in destroying a symbol of justice and fair-dealing :

Their repentance was too late : they were blotted out of the earth for the mischief they had made.

167. The task of Lot was a hard one : his mission was to people addicted to crimes abominable.

His reasoning with them was in vain : it only excited their wrath.

They threatened to cast him out, but were themselves over-whelmed in disaster.

Shu'aib had to rebuke fraud and commercial dishonesty : he met only ridicule, but the just and fair dealing he preached was vindicated in the end.

168. Thus the Truth of God must win against folly and falsehood.

The Spirit of Inspiration and faith brought down the Qur-ān to the mind of the holy Prophet,

That he might teach in noble Arabic speech, and through it reach the world.

If obstinate rebels do resist the Message, their day is brief :

With humble, gentle kindness it must make its way to all, nearest and farthest.

It is not like the vain words of poets false wandering without a goal : it is Truth, that fills the heart which trusts in God.

S. 27. 169. Revelation shows us a glimpse of the spiritual world, guides us in this life, and gives us the Hope of eternal Bliss in the Hereafter.

It works a complete transformation in us,

As it did with Moses when he saw the mystic Fire and was given the Signs with which to reclaim a people lost in superstition and sin, and proud of sin.

170. No less were David and Solomon versed in knowledge and mystic wisdom.

Even Solomon could appreciate the wisdom of the humble Ant.

He used all his power and resources in extending the Kingdom of God.

In wonderful ways did He lead the Queen of Sheba to the Light of the Faith of Unity, and confirmed her in pure worship, the worship of the Lord of the Worlds.

171. In Ṣāliḥ's pure preaching the evil Thamūd found omens of ill to themselves :

In secret they plotted to take his life, and like cowards they made a league to cover their crime with lies.

Lo ! on themselves recoiled the plot : they perished in utter ruin.

The men admonished by Lot were false to themselves : they insulted the nature given them by God, and mocked the Message of Purity.

Lo ! they were buried in a shower of brimstone !

172. God's goodness and mercy are manifest through all nature and in the heart and conscience of man.

He alone knows all : our knowledge can at best be partial.

Yet we can travel through space and time and see how Evil never prospered.

God teaches us good, but how can we see if we make ourselves blind ?

At the end of all things shall we know how small is our state, but for God's Grace :

Let us bow to His Will and accept His true guidance : Let us praise Him and trust Him—now and for ever !

S. 28. 173. God's Apostles are men, and win through good life by God's Grace and their Faith.

73

So Moses was saved from the Tyrant's wrath in infancy,

And reared in the Tyrant's own den, but gently in a mother's love.

In youth was he endowed with wisdom and knowledge, strength and the will to do right.

In sorrow or misfortune he trusted in God and opened his heart to Him.

In self-imposed exile he won love by his chivalry and confidence by Truth.

In his mission he triumphed over arrogant wrong by his meekness, patience, and Faith.

So good follows good, and Evil must fall, cursed, loathed, disgraced, and despised.

174. As with Moses, so with the Apostle Muḥammad :

Revelation was given to him, by which he knew and understood, and led men, and was kind.

He was a Mercy to men, sent by God, to warn those in sin, and, by precept and example, to bring the Light to their very doors.

Those who had spiritual eyes rejoiced, and walked in God's ancient Way, now reopened,

Valuing the things of the Spirit as God's own gifts, to be their possession for ever !

175. Material good is nothing compared to the spiritual.

In the Hereafter no plea " that others misled " will avail.

Each soul must answer for itself, whether it honoured God alone or worshipped something else, and whether it received or rejected the Teachers sent by God.

The Wisdom and Plan of God are beyond all praise :

All mercy and truth proceed from Him, and there is no other—none—besides Him.

176. Men puffed up with wealth, like Qārūn, are not pleasing to God :
For wealth is for service, not for hoarding or show.
In the midst of his pride was Qārūn swallowed up in the earth, and the earth knew him no more !
It is the righteous that attain a happy End.
Let nothing keep your eyes back from that End :
Then, and only then, shall ye reach the only Reality, the glorious Reality, which is God, Who endureth for ever !

C. 29. 177. Faith must be tested in the conflicts of practical life, but Good can never be submerged.
On the contrary God will wash off all stains from those who strive, and admit them to the Fellowship of the Righteous.
Not so the hypocrites and those who reject Faith.
Their hearts are diseased, and they will not accept the right though a Noah preached to them for a thousand years, or an Abraham reasoned with them on God's most wonderful Providence.
But the true will ever search out the Truth, and Truth will always prevail.

178. Worldly power cannot through sin defy the right, as was proved in the ministry of Lot ;
Nor can Intelligence misused stand in the place of God's Light ;
Nor can boastful insolence do aught but dig its own grave.

The strength and skill, the beauty and power, of this world's life are no more than a Spider's Web,

Flimsy before the force of the eternal verities that flow from God Supreme !

179. Proclaim the Message of God, and pray to Him for purity and guidance.

God's Revelation carries its own proofs and is recognised by men of wisdom.

Its rejecters but lose their own chances of profiting by the Truth, and attaining the Paths that lead to God's own gracious Presence !

THE FINAL END OF THINGS

S. 30. 180. Great Empires rise and fall, conquer and are conquered, as happened to Rome and Persia :

But the true Decision is with God, Who will make the righteous rejoice.

Men may see but the outward crust of things, but in truth the End of things is all-in-all.

In His own good time He will separate good from evil : Praise and glory to Him for ever !

181. God's Signs are many, and so are His Mysteries : yet each does point to His Unity, Goodness, Power, and Mercy.

There is none like unto Him.

His teaching is one, and men that split up His standard Religion are but following their own lusts.

Ungrateful are they to give part-worship to others, when all worship and praise and glory are due to Him and Him alone, in Whom we have our life and being !

182. The result of Evil is Evil.

So mischief spreads, but God will restore the balance in the End.

He did create all things pure, and will purge and purify, as He does the physical world with Winds.

Destruction awaits those that break His Harmony and Law : it will come when least expected.

Let the righteous wait and endure with constancy,

For Evil is shaky, with no faith in itself and no roots, and is doomed to perish utterly.

S. 31.   183. What is the Book of Wisdom ?

It is a Guide and a Mercy to men, and teaches them how to attain Bliss.

God's Mercies are infinite : how can men deny them ?

Luqmān the Wise taught grateful worship of the One True God, and the service of men, beginning with Parents :

Every good deed is known to God and is brought to account.

So walk in the Golden Mean, and serve Him with constancy and firmness of purpose.

184. True Wisdom sees God's boundless Bounties to man, and how all nature is made to serve man's ends.

It is due from us to know our place, discern the limits of our knowledge, and see how far above us is God's Wisdom, and His Law.

Let us not deceive ourselves.

The end of all things will come, but the When and the How are known to God alone, to Whom be all Praise !

S. 32.   185. How can Unbelievers realise the Mystery of Revelation ?

They do not even see the marvel and Mystery of Time and God's Creation, and how they were themselves Created !

If they could but see how the End will shape itself,—how the Good will be sorted out from Evil !

The two are not equal in Goal.

Clear are the Signs and the Revelation of God—in nature, history, and the Message of His living Prophets.

If they learn not now, alas ! it will be too late when Time's wings are furled.

RELIGION INCLUDES THE ORDERING OF SOCIAL AND COLLECTIVE LIFE

S. 33.   186. The issue of all things depends on God alone : we must put our trust on Him as the Guardian of all affairs.

He loves truth in all things, both great and small : call things by their right names.

If false relationships by custom or superstition do harm to men or women, shun them.

The spiritual Guide is more than Father : the ladies of his household are Mothers to the Believers—in rank, dignity, and duty.

The Guide will have to give an account, in the Hereafter, of how the Truth was received which he was charged to proclaim to men.

187. When the formidable forces of a whole Confederacy bent on destroying Islam burst upon Medina, it was God's grace that saved the Muslims.

The enemies and the Hypocrites did their best to defeat the purpose of God, but they were foiled.

In the Apostle was found the ideal Leader for the men of God,

Who became heirs to the heritage misused by enemies to Faith and the Laws of God.

188. The Prophet's household is not for worldly ends; his consorts have a place and dignity beyond ordinary women.

They must recite and proclaim the Signs of God.

For women have spiritual virtues and duties like unto men.

God decrees no unhappy wedlock: fear not to dissolve such and provide what is right and fitting for the service of God.

High is the Prophet's position, and he must order his household as best befits his work and duties.

God doth watch all things.

189. Believers should cultivate refined respect in social and spiritual life.

As the Mothers of the Faithful have to uphold their dignity, so should all women protect their honour and uphold their dignity.

The Hour will come when all Evil will be punished.

Fear God, and always speak the word that leads to Right.

Arduous is the Quest of Mankind's high and noble Destiny,—beyond the reach of other creatures:

Let man but strive in Faith, and fulfil God's Trust,—by
the grace and mercy of God.

FEATURES OF THE SPIRITUAL WORLD

S. 34. 190. God's Mercy and Power endure for ever : man
should understand and not resist God's Revelation.

Human wisdom and Power, as given to David, were only
for establishing Righteousness.

Human glory, like Solomon's, rested on slender foundations.

Sabā but enjoyed her fair and prosperous state as long as
she obeyed the Law of God, but perished for unrighteousness.

Learn, then, that the Mercy and Power, Wisdom and
Justice, of God are beyond all comparison.

Do Right and prepare for the Final Day.

191. Unfaith has no stable foundations to rest on : mis-
leaders and misled will all be responsible for their deeds.

True values are not to be judged by the seeming good of
this Life :

True Good will come to its own in the End, however
derided and scorned in the period of Trial.

Revelation and the Mission of the men of God will stand
every test.

God's Truth will endure, while falsehood will perish, and
its votaries find the door of Repentance closed in the End.

S. 35.   192. God is the source of all things : all Power, Wisdom,
Beauty, and Truth flow from Him.

It is Evil that deceives and plots in the dark.

All knowledge is with God.

The things that are good and pure and true are not as the things that are evil, deceitful, and false.

God is free of all needs : it is we that need Him : let us seek His love and live.

His Message will save us from wrong, while dark is the fate of those who reject Him.

Praise and glory to Him, the Cherisher of all !

193. Man can see by his own experience what infinite shades and grades of colour there are in nature.

So are there grades in the spiritual world.

The Good and the True understand God, Who knows and watches over all His creatures.

The Good will reach Eternal Bliss, while the Evil will find no helper.

Arrogance and plotting will be the undoing of Evil : its doom is sure, if it fails to profit by the respite granted by the All-Merciful God.

S. 36. 194. The wisdom of Revelation—the Qur-ān received through the holy Prophet—is a guide to the Straight Path, and a warning against the terrible state in which the yokes of Sin enslave us.

The righteous receive it with joy, for they believe in the Hereafter.

Behold, there was once a City, to which came two righteous men with the Gospel of Truth, but they were rejected and persecuted : they were joined by a third.

But the City refused to believe or to turn from iniquity.

Only one man was found in its outskirts, to bear witness to Truth, Faith, and Righteousness, and he did suffer martyrdom.

He attained Peace, but mourned for his people, in that they shut the gates of Salvation and God's Mercy on themselves.

Alas for man's short-sighted folly in defying the Grace that would shield and deliver him !

195. Are there not Signs enough around you to bear witness to God, and His saving Grace ?

The earth dies and revives : there are mysteries of Life and Sex, of Light and the Stars and Planets in heaven, that follow their orbits by Law and in harmony !

There are the ships and the modes of transport by which man can conquer the forces around him with God-given Gifts !

Learn the Law of Goodness from them and believe in the Hereafter : it will come when least expected. Be prepared for God !

196. When the Day comes, men will be taken aback. The judgment-seat will be established.

Blessed will be those who attain Salvation.

Their Joy, Satisfaction, and Peace will be crowned with nearness to their Lord !

Alas for the Sinful, who deliberately followed Evil : their own nature and actions will speak against them :

They will face the realities of Punishment !

Both Revelation and Nature are eloquent in instructing man for his own good in the Hereafter, which will come as a certainty.

Praise and Glory to God !

37. 197. God is One, the Source and Centre of all affairs,

And we must work, in discipline, harmony, and unity to put down Evil.

The Hereafter is sure, when personal responsibility will be enforced.

For the true and sincere servants of God, there will be the highest Bliss, unmixed and everlasting :

For those who defy God's Law there will be the deepest enduring Misery.

Which will men choose ?

198. The Prophets of God formed a series that worked in God's service to instruct their fellow-men.

In case of distress God helped and delivered them.

Men did flout and persecute them, but they carried out their mission with constancy ; and God's Purpose always won, to the destruction of Evil.

So was it in the story of Noah and the Flood, of Abraham the True, of Ismā'īl ready for self-sacrifice, of Isaac the righteous, of Moses and Aaron, of Elias and Lot :

All men of Faith, who receive the blessings of posterity, and Peace and Salutation from God Most Gracious.

199. So was it also with Jonah ; he had his trials, but God had mercy on him, and his mission was successful.

How can men ascribe to God qualities and relations derogatory to His nature ? High is He above all creatures.

The ranks of angels and apostles stand firm in His service.

Evil is sure to be overcome.

So Praise and Glory to God, the Lord of Honour and Power, and Peace to His Apostles !

S. 38.   200. Self-glory and Separatism, these are among the roots
of Evil, also Envy and Suspicion.

Not all the combinations of Evil can for a moment reverse
God's Purpose or His Justice.

David, endowed with worldly Power and the Virtues, had
yet to purge himself of the thought of Self-glory, which
he did ; and thus he became one of those nearest to God.

201. For just ends was the world created.

Solomon, in the midst of his worldly power and glory,
never forgot God ;

Nor Job in the midst of afflictions ;

Nor other men of Power and Vision, whose patience and
constancy brought them nearer to God.

So should all the righteous strive to win the final Bliss,
for truly grievous are the woes of Evil in the Final Account.

202. The Gospel of Unity is the true Cure for Evil :

For it gives the good news of God's Power Supreme, and
His Mercy and Forgiveness again and again.

It warns us to avoid Evil, for Evil arose from selfish Pride
and Rebellion.

No power has it over God's servants, sincere and true :

While Revelation comes as a gift free to all God's Creation.

S. 39.   203. To God is due sincere devotion, and to Him alone :
there is none like unto Him.

All nature obeys His laws, and our own growth and life
proclaim Him Lord and Cherisher.

How can we blaspheme ?

We must serve Him, the One, the True, with sincere devotion, and follow His Law in its highest meaning : or else the loss is our own.

All nature proclaims aloud His Grace and Loving-kindness.

204. What distance separates the man whose heart is melted by the Message of God and enlightened by His Light, and him who rejects Revelation !

God teaches men by Parables : straight is His Word and clear.

Any doubts in the minds of men will be resolved after Death :

Even now, God's Signs are enough : no other can guide.

Death and his twin-brother, Sleep, are in the hands of God : to Him is our Goal. He will judge in the End.

His Will is all-in-all. No other thing can be of any account before His Law.

205. But no soul need be in despair because of its sin : God's Forgiveness and Mercy are unbounded.

Turn to God in repentance now, for at Judgment it will be too late.

Unity in worship and life is commanded by God. Go not astray.

When Judgment comes, it will be a new World.

In perfect justice will the followers of Evil be sorted out from the Good.

And the righteous will rejoice, singing praises to God with the angels on high.

S. 40.   206. Believe in God, for He is Perfect in Knowledge and Power, forgives Sin and accepts Repentance, and justly enforces His Law.

Those who reject Him are but in deceit : His glory is sung by the highest and purest.

Give all devotion to Him alone.

The Day of Requital is ever drawing near, when Falsehood will vanish and God's Truth and Justice will be established for all Eternity.

207. Travel in space and time, and you will see that Evil came to nothing but evil.

Mighty men of old in arrogance plotted against God's Truth, but were brought low.

A humble Believer in Pharaoh's Court stood up for Truth, and counselled his People to obey the Right :

In earnest humility did he address them ; they heard him not.   But he was saved and they were engulfed in the Wrath of God.

208. God's grace and help are ever ready for His servants who patiently persevere.

Let not arrogance blind the souls of men : the Hour of Judgment is bound to come.

The keys of Life and Death are in the hands of God.

Dispute not the Signs of God, but learn from History and the world around you.

Science and skill avail you not if the soul is dead.

S. 41.   209. Revelation explains, and makes things clear ; it gives the message of hope and mercy, and it warns men against the snares of Evil.

Deny not God, the Lord of the Worlds, Whose glory and power are shown in Creation, and His Mercy in Revelation.

Learn from the fate of the Peoples of old !

Learn from the warnings of your own nature : your very limbs and faculties, if misused, bear witness against you.

Repent ere it be too late.

210. The best of men is the man of Faith, who calls all men to share his Faith,

Whose life is pure, and whose law of life is the Will of God.

Eschew all evil, and adore God, and Him alone.

His Signs are everywhere, and His Message is the same through all the ages, a guide and a healing to those who believe.

Dispute not, but live righteousness.

Knowledge belongs to God, but Falsehood deprives man of hope, humility, and clear sight, and drives him to hypocrisy.

So turn to Truth, and live.

S. 42.   211. Inspiration is part of the Glory and Goodness of God.

His Unity is shown in His Creation ; yet man will turn to false gods, and dispute about Religion.

Faith has been one at all times, but sects and divisions rose through selfish contumacy.

Let all contention cease, and conduct weighed by the just balance of God's Word.

The just and the unjust will be brought before God, Whose Mercy and Bounty are writ large in the Signs in His marvellous Creation,—one, yet diverse !

212. What we call the ills of life is due to our own ill-deeds, and many of them are forgiven by God.

His Plan can never be frustrated.

This Life is but a stage of convenience : live true and resist all wrong, but learn the best way to do so.

On God rely ; else no protector will you find.

God's Revelation comes as a Guide and Mercy : it shows the Straight Way, the Way of God All-Wise.

S. 43. 213. Revelation makes everlasting Truths clear : those who mock merely undo themselves.

Consider the Signs of God's gracious kindness around you, and glorify Him :

Attribute not unworthy qualities nor any companions to the One True God.

Seek Truth in worship more than mere ancestral ways, and shut not out Revelation's Light.

214. If the Arabs hark back to ancestry, why not accept the Faith of Abraham the True ?

He joined not gods with God.

Spiritual worth is measured by other things than gold or silver or the adornments of this world. These are but things of the hour.

The lasting gifts are those of the Hereafter.

If Israel goes back to Moses, how he was mocked by Pharaoh in his pride of power !

Yet Pharaoh and his deluded people perished : so ends the pomp and power and vanity of this world !

215. If Christians go back to Jesus, he was but a man and a servant of God :

He came to still the jarring sects, not to create a new one : he preached the One True God, his Lord.

So give up disputing, and join in devotion to God.

That is the Way to the Garden of Bliss, but the opposite leads to the Fire.

Beware ! the Truth has come, and God knows how you receive it.

He is the Lord of Power and Mercy.

The Truth must prevail : resist it not.

S. 44. 216. Blest is the night in which God's Message comes down, as a Mercy to men, to warn them against Evil.

How fractious of men to ignore or suppress such warnings ?

Proud Pharaoh and his Chiefs did resist God's authority, but their sins rebounded on themselves :

They were swallowed up by the sea ; and their tilth, their gardens, their noble fanes and buildings, and all the advantages of which they boasted, passed to other hands.

Not a tear was shed over them in heaven or earth.

Thus ends the tale of power misused.

217. So with the Children of Israel : granted gifts and favours, they became arrogant and fell.

Can the Quraish escape the doom for sin ?

We created the world for just ends.

The day will come when good and evil will be sorted out : each will meet the fruits of its own deeds.

Give good heed to the Message revealed, and wait and watch.

S. 45. 218. The Signs of God are everywhere : His power, wisdom, and goodness are shown through all Creation and in Revelation.

How can man be so ungrateful as to reject true Guidance reaping thus the fruits of Evil ?

But men of Faith have patience and forgive their weaker brethren, and trust in the final justice of God.

Form no sects, as was done aforetime, nor make your lusts your gods :

The Future is sure, and in the hands of God, to Whom all will bend the knee, when Truth will shine in all its glory.

So praise and glory to God, the Lord and Cherisher of all the worlds !

S. 46. 219. Creation is for just ends, and Falsehood is but straying from the Path :

Say what people may, truth carries its own vindication : follow it firmly.

Let age think of youth, and youth not turn rebellious.

There are fine gradations in the kingdom of God : then strive for the best.

Let not pride and arrogance undo you : the humble are often the best recipients of Truth.

All will come right in good time : so persevere with patient firmness of purpose.

Justice that seems to tarry comes really on swiftest foot but sure.

S. 47.   220. No plots against Truth or Faith will succeed : but those who follow both will be strengthened.

Be firm in the fight, and God will guide.

Rebellion against God is destruction : fidelity will cool the mind and feed the heart ; it will warm the affections and sweeten life.

Hypocrisy carries its own doom.

221. Those eager for service want the call for service ; but the hypocrites blench at such call.

If it were not obeyed, and evil should get the upper hand, will it not stalk arrogant over the land, and trample underfoot all claims of right and kinship ?

Fight it, and fail not in the test of your mettle.

Be bold and establish the Flag of Righteousness in the highest places.

Thus comes Peace, for which due sacrifice must be made.

S. 48.   222. Victory and Help go with calmness of mind, faith, fidelity, zeal, and earnestness, not with greed, lukewarmness, or timidity.

Discipline and obedience are essential for service.

The rewards for service are not to be measured by immediate results, but accrue in countless hidden ways to Patience and Restraint.

Be strong against Evil, but kind and gentle amongst yourselves : the seed will grow and become strong, to your wonder and delight.

S. 49.   223. Respectful behaviour to the Leader, in manner, voice, and demeanour, are the bonds and cement of an organised community.

The whispers of rumour should be tested, and selfish impatience should be curbed to discipline.

All quarrels should be composed, if necessary by the force of the community, but with perfect fairness and justice.

Ridicule, taunts, and biting words, should be avoided, in presence or in absence.

Suspicion and spying are unworthy of men who believe.

All men are descended from one pair : their honour depends, not on race, but on righteousness.

Faith is not a matter of words, but of accepting God's Will and striving in His Cause.

The coming into Islam confers no favour on others, but is itself a favour and a privilege, a guidance for those who are true and sincere.

FINAL ADJUSTMENT OF TRUE VALUES

S. 50.   224. The Apostle's credentials are the Revelation he brings.

Let them not wonder at the Message or at the News of the Hereafter.

They have but to look at the starry heavens and at Nature around them to see God's goodness and His power to bring life out of the dead, and to punish all wrong.

Every deed, word, and thought are in the eternal Record.

Death will open your eyes and make you see Realities.

Then will every action bear its due fruit, and no soul can shift its responsibility on to another.

225. As Goodness has possibilities unlimited, so has Evil in the opposite direction.

To those who bring a heart unsullied and to God devoted, will be Peace, Security, and Eternal Life—the Rays from God's own Presence.

Adore ye God and pay no heed to whispers of Doubt and Evil : these must vanish at Judgment, when Truth and Justice reign Supreme.

S. 51. 226. Various are the ways of working we see in God's world,—strong and gentle, scattering and uniting :

Through it all runs a Purpose true and stable, which we shall see fulfilled on the Day of Judgment and Justice, which must inevitably come to pass :

Give up false doctrines, which agree not among themselves or with facts.

For evil must end in evil, and good in joy and felicity.

The good worship God and serve God's creatures : those needing help are ever in their thoughts.

They see Signs of God in all things in heaven and earth, and in their own hearts and minds.

227. Even Abraham the True had need to be told before he could realise the purpose of God.

Clear Signs were sent for warning, as, of old, to Pharaoh, the 'Ād, the Thamūd, and the people of Noah, and the warning inevitably came to pass.

Our Signs are for your instruction. Heed them and learn by them.

Those who believe find profit in their lives :

Those who reject or deny,—alas ! they learn not from the past. Woe unto them ! The loss is their own !

S. 52. 228. By the sacred Symbols—of the Mount Sublime, the Eternal Record on an open scroll, the House of Worship thronged with men, the Canopy blue of unfathomed heights, and the boundless Ocean with its resistless tidal Swell,—all acts of men must have their inevitable fruits.

New worlds will be born with the Day of Doom : new values established by God's Decree.

Consumed will be Evil in the fire of Reality :

And Good will come to its own—in personal and social Bliss, but most in the full realisation that God is good, the Beneficent, the Merciful . . .

Proclaim, then, the praises of the Lord, nor heed the slanders of Ignorance or spite :

For the Lord Who created will cherish ; His Plan will overthrow the puny plots of men.

Hold firm with patience in Faith in the Hereafter, and sing His praises even in the busy marts of this world,

But chiefly in the stillness of the Night and the holy hour of Dawn as the Stars retreat, singing glory to the Maker of their own most glorious Sun.

S. 53. 229. True revelation is not a process either of error or deception, nor does the Prophet speak from himself as he desires.

It is God's inspiration, true, without doubt.

It is reality,—the inner reality of heaven as far as knowledge can reach,

Not the false ideas and idols that men construct for themselves, names without truth behind them.

The goal of all things is God, as He is the One from Whom starts Reality.

No other can e'er intercede except as He wills.

He made us, and knows all that we are.

It is not for us to justify ourselves, but to offer ourselves as we are.

230. When once in God's Way, turn not away, nor check your generous impulse to give your all to God.

The spiritual world unseen is above all worldly bargains.

Each soul must bear its own responsibility. It must strive its utmost and attain its end.

The final Goal of all is God:

In His hands are Laughter and Tears, Life and Death, the mystery of Birth and Creation, and the Hereafter.

He controls our Bliss and inner satisfaction.

He is Lord of the highest and noblest in Nature.

His hand traces the course of History.

Learn, oh learn from His Revelation, and adore the Lord of your inmost Soul!

. 54. 231. With every breath of our life, comes nearer and nearer the Hour of Judgment:

The proud will be brought low: the lovers of ease will find themselves in hardship.

Come! is there any that will truly receive admonition?

So said Noah, but his people rejected the warning and perished.

We have made our Revelation easy to understand and follow.

Is there any that will truly receive admonition?

So said the prophets of 'Ād and Thamūd; so said the prophets deputed to the People of Lot and of Pharaoh: but the wicked continued in sin and defiance and perished.

Will the present generation learn wisdom by warning? Alas! Is there any that will truly receive admonition? The Righteous will dwell in their Gardens of Bliss,—

In the joyful Assembly of realised Truth, in the Presence of their Sovereign Most High!

S. 55.　232. God's creatures! Which favours of God will ye deny?

Most Gracious is God, Who reveals Himself in the Qur-ān, in man's Intelligence, and in the nature around man.

Balance and Justice, Goodness and Care, are the Laws of His Worlds.

Created from clay, man can yet comprehend the Lord of the Easts and the Wests, Him who sustains all His creatures,

Him Who bestows the Jewels of Life and Faith,

Him Who abides when all else perisheth,

Him Whose Eternity is the Hope of man's Future,

The Lord Everlasting of Justice and Glory and Bounty and Honour!

Which, then, of the favours of your Lord will ye deny?

233. Let not Evil think that it will escape Justice: its tell-tale Mark is on those who follow it, and it must meet its Reward in the final adjustment.

But the Good, the Righteous, must reach their fulfilment in the Gardens of Bliss, where every Delight will be theirs in Beauty and Dignity.

How can such Delights be pictured in words ? In symbols subjective let each take his choice.

For Good can there ever be any Reward other than Good ?

Beautiful sights and sounds, delicious fruits to nourish the soul, and Companionship where Grace is mingled with Love, may figure forth our Bliss.

Blessed be God, full of Majesty and Bounty.

God's creatures ! what favours of God will ye deny ?

S. 56. 234. The Event Inevitable is the Day of Judgment :

The world as we know it will be shaken to its depths, and its place will be taken by a world made new, where Good will be sorted out from Evil.

In Dignity and Bliss will the Good find Fulfilment :

Both those Nearest to the Throne of God and those who earned, by faith and good life, the title, Companions of the Right Hand.

Who can tell of the Misery in which the Companions of the Left Hand will live ?

They will be as it were in a fierce blast of Fire ; their drink but boiling water ; their shade that of Black Smoke that chokes their lungs ;—ever burning with hunger and thirst, and never satisfied : fit emblems of the Life in Death to which Evil leads.

235. Learn ye then to witness the Truth in your lives.

Your own creation and growth, the seeds that ye sow in the ground, the Circuit of Water through streams, rivers, and seas, to vapour, clouds, and rain that feeds the streams, the Fire that stands as an emblem of Life and Light,—all point to your Lord Supreme.

His Revelation conveys the same Message to the pure in heart.

Will ye receive it and live, assured of the truth of the Hereafter ?

Glory and Praise to God the Beneficent, Supreme in Justice, Mercy, and Truth !

HOW TO STRENGTHEN THE SOCIETY OF ISLAM

S. 57. 236. God is all-in-all : follow His Law and His Light, and obey His Apostle, who invites you to deeds of goodness and charity.

Strive and spend your resources and yourselves in the Cause of God :

He will grant you a Light to go before you and guide you to your Eternal Goal, where no Evil can enter.

When success crowns your efforts, even then is the time to humble yourselves before God, in sincere witness to His Love.

The pleasures here below are deceptive : be foremost in seeking God and His Good Pleasure :

Trust Him : be not like those who mistook mere renunciation of the world for God's service.

God's Grace is for all : be your love and your service for all.

S. 58. 237. Let not false pretences or superstitions degrade the position of woman.

Eschew secret plottings and secret counsels.

Observe order and decorum in public assemblies, and seek not in selfish pride to engage your Leader's private attention.

It is wrong to turn to the enemies of God for friendship : they make their oaths a cloak for wrong-doing, and keep back men from the Right.

But none can resist the Power or the Judgment of God.

The Righteous seek only His Good Pleasure, and rejoice therein as their highest Achievement.

S. 59. 238. God's wisdom foils the treachery of men, and makes the path smooth for Believers who strive even against odds.

Against God's decrees all resistance is vain.

In property taken from the enemy, let those in need have a share, and those who sacrifice their all for the Cause.

But those who lend a helping hand in the hour of need do it for love and crave no reward, nor feel the least envy or jealousy.

They all rejoice that the Brotherhood should thrive.

Not so the Hypocrites : they are false even among themselves.

Perdition is the end of all evil.   But the Good and Faithful will achieve felicity.

Such is the power of Truth and God's Revelation.

God !   There is no god but He !—the Good, the Glorious, the Irresistible !

All Creation sings His praise,—the Exalted in Might, the Wise !

S. 60. 239. What social relations should you hold with men whose hearts are filled with rancour,—who hate both God and men of God ?

Surely you cannot offer love and friendship to such as seek to destroy your Faith and you.

Seek protection for you and yours from God and not from God's sworn enemies.

But deal kindly and justly with all : it may be that those who hate you now may love you : for God can order all things.

But look not for protection to those who are bent on driving you out.

Let not believing women be handed over to Unbelievers : no marriage tie is lawful between them.

When women wish to join your society, take their assurance that they yield not to sin or unbeseeming conduct.

Take every care to keep your society free and pure, and self-contained.

S. 61. 240. God's glory shines through all the universe.

What deeds of unity and discipline, of love and righteousness, have you to show in conduct ?

Or do you only mock and insult the apostles as they did of old ?

Nay, trust in God and strive your utmost in His Cause.

Little have you to give, but glorious is the reward that God will give you,—now and in the Eternal Life to come !

S. 62. 241. God's care for His creatures is universal.

His Revelation is for all—ignorant and lowly as well as learned and high-placed,—now and for ever.

None can arrogantly claim exclusive possession of God's gifts :

If they do, search their hearts within, and you will find them afraid of Death and Judgment.

Men of Faith ! On the Day of Assembly, when you hear the call, hasten earnestly to answer it : leave off business, and join in common worship and devotion.

Then you may disperse about your ordinary business, but remember the Praises of God always :

It is He alone that can provide for your every need, and His gifts are best.

S. 63. 242. The Oaths of Hypocrites are a screen for their misdeeds.

They think they deceive with their fair exteriors and plausible talk, but their minds are impervious to the real Truth.

They may plot to withhold from men of God such things of this world as they may command ;

They may plot to expel and persecute the righteous ; they may call them ill names and slight them.

But to God belong the treasures of the heavens and the earth, and He will bestow according to His wise and universal Plan.

Let not the world's foolish craze divert the Believers from the service of God—from good deeds and Charity.

Now is the time : all vain will be your pleas and your regrets when the shadow of Death cuts off your last chance of Repentance !

S. 64. 243. The self-same God created all men.

If some do good and others evil, and ye wonder how the good do suffer and the evil thrive, remember the Final Goal, when true adjustments will be made.

The Gainers here will be the Losers there, and the Losers Gainers.

Some of this exchange you will see even here, in this life, for Unbelievers who deny the Hereafter ;

But in the Hereafter, full account and true adjustment of good and ill will follow before the Judgment-Seat :

Nay, Good will get more than its full reward :

For God is Bounteous, Merciful, Mighty, Wise.

S. 65. 244. Guard well your truth and pure integrity in sex relations.

Keep the tie of marriage sacred ;

But where it must be dissolved, use all precautions to ensure justice to the weaker party and protect the interests of unborn or new-born lives as well as social decency ;

And close not to the last the door of reconciliation.

God's Laws must be obeyed : 'tis man's own loss if he is deaf to the Voice which teaches him, or blind to the Light which guides him.

God's universe of beauty and wonder stands strong in wisdom : Let man but tune himself thereto.

S. 66. 245. The relations between the sexes are embittered by misunderstandings and conflicts that produce unhappiness and misery, personal and social.

Harmony and confidence are due between the sexes,

Not disgust or isolation, which may please some but cause injustice to others.

Respect each other's confidence, and if you fail, repent and make amends.

The good man seeks virtue for himself and his family.

If Evil is yoked to Good it must take the fruit of its own deeds ; the worldly tie will profit naught ;

But Good should firmly make a stand, and will be saved, for God doth care for all His true devoted Servants.

S. 67. 246. Lordship in right and in fact belongs to God Most
Gracious, Whose Goodness and Glory and Power are writ
large on all His Creation.

The beauty and order of the Heavens above us proclaim
Him.

Then who can reject His Call but those in pitiful delusion ?

And who can fail to accept, that truly knows himself and
the mighty Reality behind him ?

The earth and the good things thereof are prepared for man
by his Gracious Lord, Who guards him from hourly dangers.

Who sustains the wonderful flight of the Birds in mid-air ?

Above, and below, and in mid-air can we see His boundless
Signs.

We know that His Promise of the Hereafter is true.

The spring and source of the goodness of things is in Him,
and will appear triumphant when the Hour is established.

S. 68. 247. The Pen is the symbol of the permanent Record, the
written Decree, the perfect Order in the government of the
world.

And by that token, the man of God comes with a Plan and
guidance that must win against all detraction.

Truth is high above Slander.

But men must be tried against selfishness and overweening
confidence in themselves, such as would lead them to forget
God and His providence,—

Like the brothers who built castles in the air about their
garden and found it desolate in one night's storm.

But repentance brought them forgiveness : thus work the
Wrath and the Mercy of God.

248. To evil and good there can never be the same end :
No authority can the unjust produce for their false imagi-
nings.

In shame will they realise this on the Day when all illusions
will vanish and they find that the time for repentance is past.

The good man should wait and should never lose patience,
even though things go dead against him.

Jonah suffered in agony, but his sincere repentance brought
him the grace of his Lord, and he joined the company of the
Righteous ;

For Truth is firm and unshaken, is calm and works good,
through all God's Creation.

S. 69.   249. In this fleeting world few things are what they seem.
What then is sure Reality ?

Nations and men in the past assumed arrogance and
perished because they were unjust,

But that destruction was but a foretaste of the Doom to
come in the Hereafter, when all Creation will be on a new
plane, and true values will be fully established :

To the Righteous will be bliss, and to Evil, Punishment.

The Word of Revelation is not a Poet's imagination or a
Soothsayer's groping into the future.

It is God's own Message, of Mercy to the Righteous, and
warning to those who reject the Truth.

Praise and glory to the name of God Most High !

S. 70.   250. Man can ascend to the Presence of God, but by gradual
Ways and in process of Time.

But what is Time ? A Day is as fifty thousand years on
two different planes.

What seems near is far, and what seems far is near.

So will be Judgment, when things as we know them will be transformed completely in a world all new.

Evil will come to its own, whatever its masks in this transitory world, and good will surely reach its goal.

The good life is patient, in prayer and well-doing, Faith, and the earnest search for the Good Pleasure of God, purity and probity.

These are the paths to the Heights and the Gardens of Bliss. No evil can enter there :

For the evil are other ways, leading by a steep descent to dark Ignominy !

S. 71. 251. The Prophet's Message, as was that of Noah, is a warning against sin, and the Good News of Mercy through the door of Repentance :

For God is loving and long-suffering, and His Signs are within us and around us.

But the sinners are obstinate : they plot against Righteousness, and place their trust in futile falsehoods.

They will be swept away, and the earth will be purged of Evil.

Let us pray for Mercy and Grace for ourselves, for those nearest and dearest to us, and for all who turn in faith to God, in all ages and all countries, and among all Peoples.

S. 72. 252. Spiritual Truth finds its lodgment in all sorts of unexpected places, and in all sorts of unexpected ways.

The man of God, when most depressed by the buffets of a world steeped in selfishness, sees a glorious vision :

Hidden spiritual forces work for him, make known the

truth in marvellous ways, and proclaim the Goodness and judgment of God.

They reject all Error and lead others to purify their wills and come to God.

Behold ! Every place and time, every gift is meet for the service of God, the One, the True, Whose Word the righteous one proclaims and must proclaim at all cost.

Man's duty is plain, but in the Kingdom of God, through God's chosen ones, we rise to higher and higher Mysteries as may be expedient for us.

Yet when or how our End may be, is not given to man to know :

Let him but take the Treasures well-guarded, that come to him, and praise the Lord of all Knowledge and Wisdom !

S. 73. 253. Devote yourself to the service of God in the stillness of the night, but not all night.

In the world's persecution rely on God, Who will deal with His enemies fittingly.

(*Note to S. 72.* It was two years before the Hijrat, when the Prophet, despised and rejected in his native city of Mecca, went to evangelise the lordly men of Ṭāif. They maltreated him and nearly killed him ; what caused him even greater pain was the maltreatment of the humble and lowly men who went with him. Ṭabarī has handed down that memorable Prayer of faith and humility which he offered in the midst of his suffering. On his return journey to Mecca, a glorious vision was revealed to him,—hidden spiritual forces working for him,—people not known to him accepting his mission while his own people were still rejecting him. Within two months some strangers from Medina had privately met him and laid the foundations of that Hijrat which was to change the fate of Arabia and the course of world-history.)

Let not God's service be a matter of difficulty to you :
Do all your duties in whole-hearted remembrance of God,
and ever seek His bountiful Grace.

S. 74.   254. The Seer, by devotion and contemplation, prepares
himself for the duties of Guide and Leader to mankind :

But when there comes the clear Call, he must stand forth
and proclaim the Message,—in purity, unselfish devotion, and
patience, long-suffering ;—

To save men from the Distress of the Final Day.

For many there be who glory in a life of ease and plenty,
arrogant splendour, and the applause of men,

Who scorn God's Truth and reject the divine.

How will they fare when the Judgment comes, and the
Penalty ?

Every Fact in Life's grand Pageant is but a Portent for the
Future.

Every soul is in pledge and must redeem itself by Faith and
Prayer, by charity and earnest care for the Realities of life.

Bring but the will, and God will guide,—the Lord of
Righteousness, the Lord of Mercy and Forgiveness !

S. 75.   255. Eschew all Evil : for man was not created without
purpose or without responsibility.

The Day of Account will come, and his own Conscience
bears witness that he must walk straight ; for he must face
that Day's Realities.

With patience await the unfoldment of God's wise Purpose.
Keep the Hereafter ever in view.

The faces of the Blest will beam with brightness and beauty.

For the others, Death will be a terror,—for duties neglected and sins committed.

Woe unto man that he thinks not now of God's Purpose and the noble Destiny for which God gave him Life and its Gifts.

S. 76. 256. Man was evolved out of nothing, and through low beginnings ; but he was given Insight and Understanding.

God showed him the Way ; and if man doth wilfully reject the Right, man but chooses Chains and Yokes and a Blazing Fire within his own soul.

Not so the Devotees of Right : they attain the Mystic Fountain of Kāfūr :

For, purely out of love for God, they do good to God's Creatures, and serve them.

The Light of Beauty and Joy will be on them.

In full felicity and honour will they live in the Garden of Delights, and share in the Banquet—the Presence and Glory Divine !

$$\star \qquad \star \qquad \star$$

The Righteous are patient in Constant Devotion :

God's Way is open to all : whosoever has the Will, may attain to the Perfect Goal.

S. 77. 257. The winds in the world of nature are types of God's Bounty and Power :

They gently bring the beneficent rain, and when roused to wrath, they clean the world and wipe out Infection.

So works God's Revelation, in sunshine and storm.

It will root out Evil, and restore true values at Judgment.

Truly terrible will be that Day for the evil ones.

It will be a Day of Sorting out : ah woe, that Day, to the Rejecters of Truth !

Will man not learn from his own little story, or from nature around him ?

The blazing Fire will be indeed an enveloping Punishment.

How dreadful the contrast with the Bliss of the Righteous !

Learn ye, therefore, Humility, and approach God's Throne in Repentance and Earnest Endeavour.

THE HEREAFTER

S. 78. 258. The Great News for man, in his spiritual Destiny, is the Judgment to come, the Day of Sorting Out.

Do not the Power, the Goodness, and the Justice of God reveal themselves in all nature ?—

The Panorama around us, the voice in our souls, and the harmony between heaven and earth ?

That Day is sure to arrive at its time appointed, when behold ! the present order will pass away.

Then will the Fruits of Evil appear, and the Fruits of Righteousness.

God's blessings will be infinitely more than the merits of men can ever deserve ;

But who can argue with the Fountain of Grace ? And who can prevent the course of Justice ?

Let us then, before it becomes too late, betake ourselves to our Lord Most Gracious !

S. 79. 259. Never can Evil escape God's order and law :

His angels are ever present to bring the wicked to their bearings,

And they ever strive and press forward to bring comfort, succour, and God's Mercy to those who seek it.

Then will come the Day when the proud shall be humbled, though they deny the coming Judgment.

What happened to Pharaoh? He flouted God's Message specially sent to him, and arrogantly proclaimed: "I am your Lord Most High!"

He perished in this life and will answer for his deeds in the next.

★   ★   ★

But can ye not see, O men, the mighty works of God in the heavens and on earth?—

The darksome splendour of the Night with its Stars, and the daylight splendour of the Sun?—

How the earth, with its spacious expanse and its mountains, yields moisture and pasture, and feeds and sustains men and cattle, through God's wise Providence?

Ah! transgress not all bounds and earn not the Fire of Punishment,

But fear God and His Judgment, and prepare for the Garden of Perpetual Bliss.

Delay not! The Judgment is sure, and it's nigh!

S. 80. 260. Men not blest with the good things of this life may yet be earnest seekers of Truth and Purity,

And deserve as much attention as those who seem to wield some influence, yet who in their pride are self-sufficient.

God's Message is universal: all have a right to hear it.

Held high in honour, kept pure and holy, it should be writ by none but good and honourable men.

★   ★   ★

God's Grace is showered on man not less for his inner growth than in his outward life.

There must be a final Reckoning, when each soul must stand on its own past Record:

The faces, then, of the Blest will beam with Joy and Light,

While the Doers of Iniquity will hide in Dust and Shame and Darkness.

S. 81. 261. How can the soul's self-conviction be fitly expressed, except by types of tremendous cataclysms in nature, and still more by tremendous searchings in the heart of man?

These want deep pondering.

When once the spiritual Dawn has " breathed away " the Darkness of the Night, the Vision Glorious clears all doubts, and brings us face to face with Truth.

The highest Archangel in heaven is sent by God to bring these truths to men through their Apostle.

God's Grace flows freely: we have but to tune our Will to His,—the ever-loving Righteous God.

S. 82. 262. How fixed is the order holding together this material universe above and below us?

Yet it must give way before the vast Unfathomed Truth in which man will see his past and his future in true perspective.

To God he owes his life and all its blessings: will he not see that the Future depends on Right and Justice?

Righteousness must come to its own, and so must Discord and Rebellion.

The Day must come when Discord must finally cease, and the Peace of God and His Command are all-in-all.

S. 83. 263. Shun Fraud in all things :

In little things of daily life, but specially in those subtler forms of higher life, which will be exposed to view at Judgment, however hidden they may be in this life.

Give every one his due.

For the Record of ill deeds and good is fully kept, and the stains of sin corrupt the soul.

Reject not the Real now, nor mock :

For the time will come when the True will come to its own, and then the mighty arrogant will be abased !

S. 84. 264. All mysteries, fair or shrouded in gloom, will vanish when the full Reality stands revealed.

If this Life is but Painful toil, there's the Hope of the Meeting with the Lord !

That will be Bliss indeed for the Righteous, but woe to the arrogant dealers in sin !

Like the sunset Glow or the Shades of Night, or the Moon's ever-changing light, man's life never rests here below, but travels ever onwards stage by stage.

Grasp then God's Message and reach the Heights, to reap a Reward that will never fail through all eternity !

S. 85. 265. Woe to those who persecute Truth !

They are being watched by mighty Eyes ;—

The eyes of the Stars of the Darkness of Night, the searching shafts of the Future afar, and the men and angels of the Light within ;—

They will have to answer when Judgment comes ; and a clear Record will witness against them.

Are they cruel to men because of their Faith ?

The Fire they use will be turned against them.

For God is strong, and will subdue the mightiest foes.

Be warned, and learn from His gracious Message, preserved through all Time !

S. 86. 266. Through the darkest night comes the penetrating light of a glorious Star.

Such is the power of Revelation : it protects and guides the erring.

For what is man ? But a creature of flesh and bones !

But God by His Power doth raise man's state to a Life Beyond !—when lo ! all things hidden will be made plain.

Man's help will then be but the Word of God, which none can thwart.

So wait with gentle patience—for His Decision.

S. 87. 267. Wonderful are the ways of God in Creation,

And the love with which He guides His creatures' destinies,

Gives them the means by which to strive for maturity by ordered steps,

And reach the end most fitted for their natures.

His Law is just and easy, and His Grace is ever ready to help :

Let us look to the Eternal Goal, with hearts and souls of Purity, and glorify His name :

For in this changing, fleeting world, his Word is always true, and will remain, through all the ages, ever the same.

S. 88. 268. Have you heard of that Tremendous Day when the Good from the Evil will be separated ?

There will be Souls that Day will burn and grovel in the blazing Fire of Wrath !

No Food can fill their Hunger : no Drink, alas, can slake
their fierce Thirst !

There will be Souls that Day will shout with Joy to the
glory of their Lord !
Their past Endeavour will now be Achievement.
Raised high on Thrones of Dignity they will be guests at
the sumptuous Feast of Bliss.

Let man but look at his dominion o'er the beasts of the
field,
Or his glorious Canopy of stars,
Or the Eternal Hills that feed his streams,
Or the wide expanse of Mother Earth that nurtures him,
And he will see the ordered Plan of God.
To Him must he return and give account !
Let him, then, learn his Lesson and live.

S. 89. 269. Man is apt to forget the contrasts in nature and life,
and all that they mean in his spiritual growth.
Perchance his mind is so absorbed in what he sees, that he
doubts the vast Realities he does not see.
The Present makes him blind to the Past and to the Future.
Fooled by glory, he fears not a fall ;

(*Note*. Man is easily cowed by contrasts in his own fortunes, and
yet he does not learn from them the lesson of forbearance and kindness to others, and the final elevation of goodness in the Hereafter.
When all the things on which his mind and heart are set on this
earth shall be crushed to nothingness, he will see the real glory and
power, love and beauty, of God, for these are the light of the Garden
of Paradise.)

And baulked in disaster, he gives up Hope and sometimes Faith.

Let him study Nature and History, and restore his Faith :

Realising the Sure Event, the Hereafter, let him find his fullest fulfilment in the service and the Good-Pleasure of God !

MAN'S STRUGGLES AND HIS HIGH DESTINY

90. 270. The Prophet's own City persecuted him.

Honoured by his nativity, it sought to slay him :

Yet he loved it and purged it of all that was wrong.

What toil and struggle did it not involve ?

Man is made for toil and struggle :

Let him not boast of ease and wealth.

He will be called to account for all his doings.

Let him use his God-given faculties, and tread the steep path that leads to Heaven's Heights :

The steps thereto are Love, unselfish Love, given freely to God's creatures—all those in need—and Faith in God, and Patience joined with self-restraint and kindness.

Thus only can we reach the ranks of the blest Companions of the Right Hand !

91. 271. All nature around us and her pageants, and the soul of man within, proclaim the goodness of God.

God gave the soul the power of choice and the sense of Right and Wrong.

Let man keep it pure and attain Salvation,—soil it with sin and reach Perdition.

Inordinate wrong-doing ruined the Thamūd.

They defied God's sacred Law and His prophet, and went to Destruction for their crime.

272. When we consider God's wonderful Creation, we see many mysteries—many opposites—many differences;

The succession of nights and days, the creation of male and female.

Can we wonder at the differences in the nature and objectives of man?

He is endowed with Will, and he must strive for the Right through all his diverse paths.

For the righteous the way is made the smoother for Bliss;

For the arrogant crooked will, the way is the smoother for Misery.

But God's guidance is always nigh, if man will choose it.

And what is the goal for those who choose aright?—

The sight of the Face of God Most High: for that indeed is happiness supreme.

273. What an example we have in the Prophet's life!

When moments of inspiration were still, his soul yet felt the power of that stillness,

Like one who prays by night and waits for the dawn, knowing how the light grows brighter every hour till noon,

And well content that night and morn and the hours succeeding are but steps to the plenary splendour of noon.

He was content and consoled in the thought that God had bestowed His loving care on him in the past, and so the future was sure.

He followed the Light Divine,—

To help the helpless, to attend with patience to the call of those in need, and to rehearse and proclaim and share the boundless Bounties of God!

274. The Prophet's mind and heart had indeed been expanded and purified ;

The burden which pressed on his soul had been removed ;
And his name exalted in this world and the next.

For the righteous man there is no trouble but is linked with ease and joy :

He must strive at every stage, and look to God alone as the goal of all his hopes.

275. Nature and history and the Light of Revelation, through the ages, show

That man, created by God in the best of moulds, can yet fall to the lowest depths,

Unless he lives a life of faith and righteousness.

Then will he reach his goal :

If not, he must stand his Judgment—none can doubt— before the wisest and justest of Judges.

276. Noble is the mission of the Prophet, selected to proclaim the Message of God,

The Lord and Cherisher of all His Creation, whose measureless bounties include the instruction of man in new and ever new knowledge.

But alas for man ! he fancies himself self-sufficient,

Turns away from the Path, and misleads others.

But nothing is hidden from God.

He will bring all untruth and sin and rebellion to Judgment, and subdue all evil.

The righteous bow in adoration to God, and draw closer to Him.

S. 97.   277.   Blessed indeed is the Night of Power !—

When the Mercy of God's Revelation breaks through the darkness of the human soul !

All the Powers, of the world divine, speed on their mystic Message of Mercy, by God's command,

And bless every nook and corner of the heart !

All jars are stilled in the reign supreme of Peace,

Until this mortal night gives place to the glorious day of an immortal world !

S. 98.   278.   But those who reject the light of Truth are obstinate.

Why should they persist in evil ways when the Clear Evidence has come before them ?

The straight Religion is simple :

To adore with a pure heart the God of Truth, to draw nigh to Him in Prayer sincere, and to serve our fellow-creatures in charity and love.

To do aught else is to fall from Grace.

But Faith and Good Life lead straight to the Goal,—

The beauteous Gardens of Bliss Eternal, and the mutual good pleasure of the Soul in her Lord.

S. 99.   279.   The Hour of Judgment must needs be heralded by a mighty Convulsion :

The Earth will give up her secrets and tell her tale of all man's doings :

Men will march in companies and clearly see the inwardness of all their Deeds :

Not an atom of Good or Evil done, but will be shown in the final Account of men convinced.

280. There are those that fight, with eager charge, the hosts of evil, and storm its citadel.

But unregenerate Man shows less than gratitude for God's most gracious bounties :

His life bears witness to his treason and his greed.

God's knowledge is all-embracing : all things hidden will be laid bare at Judgment.

281. How will the senses of man stand the Noise and Clamour of the Great Day of Account,

Whereon this life's old landmarks will vanish, and men will be helpless like scattered moths ?

Nay, but a Balance of Justice will weigh and appraise all Deeds :

And those whose good will show substance and weight will achieve a Life of good pleasure and satisfaction,

While those whose good will be light will find themselves, alas, in a blazing Pit of Punishment.

282. Be not engrossed in things ephemeral, to the neglect of higher things in life.

Life is short, and Death will soon claim you.

Oh that men would only learn, before it is too late, the serious issues of the higher life !

They must taste the consequences of their neglect.

For every good enjoyed they must in the Hereafter give a strict account.

283. Waste not, nor misuse, your life.

Time through the Ages bears witness that nothing remains but Faith and Good Deeds,

And the teaching of Truth and the teaching of Patience and Constancy.

But for these, Man against Time is in loss !

PITFALLS FOR MAN

S. 104. 284. Woe to the man or woman who deals in scandal, in word or act, or by insults or suggestions.

Woe to the backbiter, e'en if his tale is true, for the taint is in his motive.

Woe to the miser who blocks up the channels of use and service and dams up his wealth,

As if he could remain in possession for all time !

The Fire of Wrath will envelop them and wither up their hearts and minds,

And consume that largeness of life which is the portion of mankind.

S. 105. 285. Let not man be intoxicated with power or material resources :

They cannot defeat the purpose of God.

So Abraha Ashram found to his cost.

His sacrilegious attack on the holy Fane of God brought about his own undoing :

What seemed but frail destroyed his mighty hosts in a day !

(*Note.* This early Meccan Sūra refers to an event that happened in the year of the birth of our holy Prophet, say about A.D. 570. Yaman was then under the rule of the Abyssinians (Christians), who had driven out the Jewish Himyar rulers. Abraha Ashram was the Abyssinian governor or viceroy. Intoxicated with power and fired by religious fanaticism, he led a big expedition against Mecca, intend-

106. 286. Who gave the Quraish their talents for the arts of Peace, for trade and commerce, and for journeys south and north at proper seasons,

And made their home inviolable in Mecca?

Surely they, if any, should adore their Lord and listen to His Message of Unity and Truth.

107. 287. What remains if you deny all Faith and personal Responsibility?

Why then help the helpless or teach others deeds of Charity?

Vain were worship without heart and soul.

What think ye of men who make great show, but fail to meet the simple needs of daily life?

108. 288. To the man of God, rich in divine blessings, is granted a Fountain unfailing,

That will quench the spiritual thirst of millions.

Turn, then, in devotion and sacrifice to God,

Nor heed the venom of Hatred, which destroys its own hopes, alas, of the present and the future!

109. 289. The man of Faith holds fast to his faith, because he knows it is true.

ing to destroy the Ka'ba. He had an elephant or elephants in his train. But his sacrilegious intentions were defeated by a miracle. No defence was offered by the custodians of the Ka'ba, as the army was too strong for them, but it was believed that a shower of stones, thrown by flocks of birds, destroyed the invading army almost to a man. The stones produced sores and pustules on the skin, which spread like a pestilence.)

The man of the world, rejecting Faith, clings hard to worldly interests.

Let him mind his worldly interests, but let him not force his interests on men sincere and true, by favour, force, or fraud.

S. 110. 290. For that which is right the help of God is ever nigh, and victory !

When the spirit of men is stirred, they come to the flag of faith in troops and battalions.

They are to be welcomed : but Praise and Glory belong to God :

To Him we humbly turn and pray for Grace : for He is Oft-Returning in Grace and Mercy.

S. 111. 291. The Chosen One of God, in his earnest desire to proclaim the Message, gathered his kin together to hear and judge with open minds between error and truth.

Behold, the fiery " Father of Flame " blazed up with foul abuse and curses, and said to the holy one : " Perish thou ! "

With his hands he took stones and cast them at the holy one's head.

Purse-proud he headed relentless persecution.

His wife laid snares, tied thorns with twisted ropes of prickly palm-leaf fibre, and strewed them in the holy one's path on darkest nights, for cruel sport !

But lo ! the curses, insults, spite, harmed not the Innocent,

But hit the wrong-doers themselves and branded them with eternal infamy !

S. 112. 292. Keep Faith all pure and undefiled.

There is God, the One and Only ;

Eternal, Free of all needs ;
On Whom depend, to Whom go back, all things ;
He hath no son nor father nor partner.
There is no person like unto Him.

S. 113.   293. It is God Who brings forth light from darkness,
Life and activity from death,
Spiritual enlightenment from ignorance and superstition.
Banish fear, and trust His Providence.
No danger, then, from the outer world,
No secret plottings from perverted wills,
No disturbance of your happiness or good,
Can affect the fortress of your inmost soul.

S. 114.   294.   Insidious Evil lies in wait for man,
And loves to whisper and withdraw, thus testing his will.
But man can make God his sure shield ;
'Tis God who cares for him and cherishes him :
God is the heavenly King Who gives him laws ;
And God is the Goal to which he will return and be judged.
Let man but place himself in God's hands, and never can
Evil touch him in his essential inner life.

CONCLUSION

295. Thus spake, inspired, our holy Prophet, Muḥammad, on whom we invoke God's blessings for ever and ever ;—

We who are heirs to his teaching, his exemplary life, and the golden thread which he inwove into the web of human history.

In pious retreats he prayed ; much thought he gave to Life's most obstinate tangles ; 'gainst odds he strove with might and main ; wisely he led ; gently he counselled ; and firmly he subduëd Evil.

296. Mantle-clad [1] he solved the most baffling mysteries.

His soul would scale the heights of Heaven, yet showered its love on the weak and lowly of this earth.

Like a cloud that catches the glory of the Sun, he threw his protecting shade on all.

The widow's cry, and the orphan's, found an answer in his heart, as did the cry of Penury and Need.

He searched out those who felt no need, being by pride or ignorance blinded, and he fulfilled their real wants.

His last great charge summed up the rule of spiritual life in linking Faith with one universal Brotherhood.

Ah ! ne'er shall we see such life again !

[1] An epithet of mystic meaning, applied to the Prophet in the Qur-ān, S. 14, 1. I have in my mind a reminiscence of an Urdu Naʻt or Song in praise of the holy Prophet.

297. But his clarion voice still speaks his message.

His love and wisdom still pour forth without stint the inexhaustible Treasures of God, for whosoe'er will bring a purified heart to receive them.

And ne'er did the world, impoverished by its own wayward lusts and greed, need those Treasures more than now !

298. There's still with us much sorrow and sin, injustice, oppression, wrong, and hate.

Still does arrogance deaden Conscience,

Rob struggling souls of e'en the crumbs of Pity,

And make, of loathsome flesh and crumbling dust, fairseeming Idols for worship.

Still does Ignorance blow a mighty Horn and try to shame true Wisdom.

Still do men drive Slaves,—protesting smoothly the end of Slavery !

Still does Greed devour the substance of helpless ones within her power.

Nay, more,—the fine Individual Voice is smothered in the raucous din of Groups and Crowds that madly shout what they call Slogans New,—

Old falsehoods long discredited !

299. What can we do to make God's Light shine forth through the Darkness around us ?

We must first let it shine in our own true Selves !

With that Light in the niche of our inmost hearts we can walk with steps both firm and sure :

We can humbly visit the comfortless and guide their steps.

Not we, but the Light will guide !

But Oh ! the joy of being found worthy to bear the Torch, and to say to our brethren :

" I too was in Darkness, Comfortless, and behold, I have found Comfort and Joy in the Grace Divine ! "

300. Thus should we pay the dues of Brotherhood,—

By walking humbly, side by side, in the Ways of the Lord,

With mutual aid and comfort, and heartfelt prayer, backed by action,

That God's good Purpose may be accomplished in us all together !